David

from J. Germano

1979

ITALIAN POETS OF THE RENAISSANCE

Italian Poets of the Renaissance

Translated into English Verse and
with an Introduction by

JOSEPH TUSIANI

Published by
BAROQUE PRESS, INC.
Long Island City, N. Y.

ITALIAN POETS OF THE
RENAISSANCE
Copyright ©, 1971, by
JOSEPH TUSIANI

Library of Congress Catalog Card No. 72-148607

PRINTED IN THE UNITED STATES OF AMERICA BY *Theo. Gaus' Sons, Inc.*,
BROOKLYN, N. Y.

FOR GIUSEPPE RETTURA

Rorido ancora o forse un po' già sacro
al vespero bruciato
il ramo ancor visibile allo sguardo
rammenti il pio terreno dolce amato
e l'umidor gagliardo
(o gioventù felice!)
d'ogni nostra radice.

CONTENTS

FRANCESCO PETRARCA

CONTENTS—*continued*

CONTENTS—*continued*

CONTENTS—*continued*

CONTENTS—*continued*

CONTENTS—*continued*

CONTENTS—*continued*

CONTENTS—*continued*

CONTENTS—*continued*

FRANCESCO MARIA MOLZA

TEOFILO FOLENGO

VITTORIA COLONNA

CONTENTS—*continued*

PIETRO ARETINO

BERNARDO TASSO

LUIGI ALAMANNI

FRANCESCO BERNI

CONTENTS—*continued*

CONTENTS—*continued*

CONTENTS—*continued*

GASPARA STAMPA

GIAN BATTISTA GUARINI

TORQUATO TASSO

CONTENTS—*continued*

CONTENTS—*continued*

Introduction

It is not always possible to catalogue moods and feelings in a strictly chronological order. To call Dante a medieval poet is quite correct; but to call his poetry medieval is not to understand that its artistic roots are not its horizons. It was Dante who wrote in Canto III of *Purgatorio*:

> *State contenti, umana gente, al quia,*
> *ché se possuto aveste veder tutto,*
> *uopo non era parturir Maria*
>
> (Find, O you men, in the *because* your mirth,
> for, had you been allowed to see all things,
> futile it were for Mary to give birth) .

This submissive attitude, which crushes but does not ignore the incipient rebellion of man's spirit, is typically medieval. But it was also Dante who, in Canto XXVI of his *Inferno*, had already created the pre-humanistic figure of Ulysses. There is nothing medieval about Dante's Ulysses. He is the man who challenges things profane and sacred. Borne by desire to pursue valor and knowledge, he crosses the Pillars of Hercules and goes to his death only because he does not want to live "as a brute." All this might perhaps be termed pure humanism, but it is not, inasmuch as it lacks full consciousness of its own significance.

Petrarch is the first humanist in the fullness of the meaning attached to the re-evaluation of the "humus" or man's matter. With him the spirit triumphs and suffers together with the body, and the body suffers and triumphs together with the spirit. Jacopone's "lauda" in praise of all possible diseases, invoked with masochistic fervor as a new way of mortifying the body, becomes, so to speak, a parenthesis of darkness utterly absurd in the new habitat of man's light. Man's realization that there is room on earth even for his own palace is not a denial of the previous cathedral or *duomo,* but a conscious effort to restore the dignity of that very clay which God had molded in the creation of his earthly creature.

Petrarch is the first man of letters to feel the consequences of this realization. With the restlessness of his nature he studies the ancient writers not only to learn the majesty of their language but also, and above all, to find himself. But Petrarch is, first, a poet, and as such he cannot limit himself to the satisfactions of scholarly research. He sees, and feels, and reacts, as a poet. His vision does not need the aid of his humanistic discoveries; it is, instead, his humanistic fervor that, losing the selfishness of its initial aim, acquires the second nature of his poetry. Consequently, Petrarch's Laura is not Dante's Beatrice. Even love is felt in a fashion akin to the new exigencies of man's spirit. Beatrice is both the incarnation and fulfillment of Dante's mystical dream; Laura is the incarnation and fulfillment of Petrarch's spiritual and physical passion. Beatrice is angelic beauty born to redeem man's spirit; Laura is, instead, spirit and matter born to enchant and enchain matter and spirit. The two women have one thing in common—perfection; but they differ from each other in that one is an almost supernatural being, and the other is, first of all, human. This explains, or somewhat clarifies, the distance between Dante's heaven and Petrarch's earth. Ascetic aspirations and love of earthly things are easily reconciled in Dante's unshaking belief, but they find no immediate coexistence in Petrarch's soul. In his vision of the ultimate triumph of the Good, Dante had united medieval Christian faith and classical pagan thought. On the other hand, Petrarch, who does not possess the same strength and the same equilibrium, is tormented by the two contrasting feelings till his last poem and breath.

After the death of Petrarch in 1374, and of Boccaccio in 1375 (in the latter the magic of ancient Athens had found its first ardent admirer and explorer), classical erudition and search for old manuscripts were, or seemed to be, the only ecstatic ambition of the humanistic scholar. Petrarch's inner conflicts had been vented in the typically Petrarchan fashion of the secret confession (he had appropriately called *Secretum* his colloquy, both apologetic and self-tormenting, with the Saint of the *Confessions*). But when the same conflicts became external rather than internal, the confession was supplanted by the public intellectual gathering. First in the villa of the Albertis (Giovanni da Prato's *Paradiso degli Alberti* is the amusing chronicle of those varied conversations), and then in Fra Luigi Marsili's cell at Santo Spirito, the new humanists tried to reconcile religious heritage with classical culture, and divine grace with earthly beauty. Even Coluccio Salutati, the discoverer of Cicero's *Letters*, attended the meetings at Santo Spirito. More than the Augustinian spirit of the various Marsilis, it was the wealth of the monastic libraries that attracted the Florentine scholars. The example of both Petrarch and Boccaccio was more than ever alive and fruitful. But this eager return to pagan thought alarmed the zealous Dominican friar Giovanni Dominici, who began to thunder against the perils of "meretricious" books such as were placed in the hands of young men and women. His voice, however, was unable to halt or even check the high tides of the new times. Ancient books were found and studied, libraries were built, academies were born; and when, after the fall of Constantinople in 1453, Greek scholars such as Argyropulos and Calcondila were offered political asylum and academic chairs by Cosimo de' Medici, Florence became the center of the literary world, and Plato her god.

The Florentine Academy was the temple of the new religion, with Marsilio Ficino its pontiff, and Cristoforo Landino, Pico della Mirandola, Poggio Bracciolini, Lorenzo, and Politian its archpriests. In his villa of Montevecchio at Careggi Ficino translated Plato and the Neoplatonists, and his *Theologia Platonica* was to become the point of departure of almost the entire poetic production of the Renaissance.

II

Petrarchism should be studied not only as a literary phenomenon but also as a spiritual problem. As a literary phenomenon alone, it may easily be linked to the question of the language, of capital importance especially during the sixteenth century, and consequently explained as a constant effort to imitate Petrarch's elegance of expression and vitality of emotion. But such an explanation fails to tell us why so many poets, some of them not devoid of at least a spark of genius, were so enslaved by Petrarch as to be unable to express thoughts or feelings that were really their own. Seen, on the other hand, as a spiritual problem, it will immediately lay bare its soul and that of its day.

Petrarch, as we said, had been tortured by his inner conflict between spirit and matter; but he had not deemed the latter superior to the former, nor had he made of his Laura a Nencia da Barberino or of his poetry a pure poetic homage. Humanism to him had been a battle, not a scholarly exercise, and literature a conquest, not a placid *status quo*. When Petrarch's earth-for-heaven became, so to speak, earth-for-earth in the souls and in the hands of his imitators, the torment of the vacillation turned into the acquiescence of the flesh, and the spirit was no longer a motivating force but a fashionable and innocuous aspiration. From Petrarch's "uncertain pass" to Lorenzo's "uncertain morrow" the spirit of the Renaissance had deteriorated into a doubt which seemed more literary than personal. The story of a soul had become a gospel of elegance, and nothing more. All this may explain why Petrarch was turned into Petrarchism in a century which, consciously or unconsciously, had severed its links with the tragic ethical problem of Laura's poet. This may also explain why our innumerable "essayers of beds and other things" (the phrase is Carducci's) lived the most sensual life and wrote the most Platonic verse. Petrarch, too, had often quieted the restlessness of the man in more tangible sources of pleasure, but, unlike his imitators, he had also turned into true art the sincerity of his moments of repentance.

When Petrarchism became, in its second phase, merely a cult of the sonnet, even the slightest variation, or deviation, from Petrarch was to constitute matter of sacrilege. Every woman became "the only lady"; her hair had to be golden and, possibly, "with the breezes playing," and her step "an angel's gait." Cupid's arrows seemed to multiply in his magic quiver, and phoenixes and salamanders destroyed and renewed themselves in endless fire. The sonnet, a seemingly accessible and docile form, lent itself to the universal mania in a century that had nearly forgotten Dante and his *Comedy*, and could never have produced, in imitation of his engaging terza rima, poetic efforts such as Fazio degli Uberti's *Dittamondo* or Federico Frezzi's *Quadriregio*. As the fourteen-line mold seemed to be at everyone's disposal, so was the "Petrarchino," or a miniature edition of the first *Canzoniere*, in every library and every parlor. Even the countless Lauras of the Renaissance, not entirely satisfied with the languorous sonnets left by their lovers on their green-velveted desks, were eager to climb the common Parnassus on the easy wings of the Platonic fashion. Austere widows like Vittoria Colonna, Veronica Gambara, and Barbara Torelli, and merry courtesans like Gaspara Stampa, Veronica Franco, and Tullia d'Aragona, both inspired and wrote sonnets, songs, and madrigals. Bembo, the prince of all Petrarchists, and all the other poets, artists, and musicians, sought and found sanctuary in the comforting warmth of those parlors. It was the century when the suicide of fair Imperia, the most beautiful courtesan of Rome (Archbishop Bandello has left us an accurate description of her house), deeply saddened the literary world, and when, on the other hand, the death of a Cecchino Bracci, a handsome lad of fifteen, was mourned in verse and prose by at least a half dozen men of letters.

In his sonnet, "An Enigma," Edgar Allan Poe expressed in a comical and effective simile his opinion of "Petrarchan stuff" in general and "tuckermanities" in particular. But Henry Constable had already captured and explained in one of his charming sonnets to his lady the fundamental character of Petrarchism:

> *Lo! why th' Italians, yet which never saw thy rays,*
> *To find out Petrarch's sense such forged glosses try.*

Through such "forgèd glosses" the true sense of Petrarch was introduced to the rest of Europe. Wyatt and Surrey in England, Du Bellay and Ronsard in France, and Boscán and Garcilaso de la Vega in Spain, were first to trace the clear and vital sources of the various and no more limpid currents of Petrarchism. The Italian customs were the butt of foreign satire, but the Italians were still the masters of poetry. In his "Epístola satírica y censoria," addressed to Don Gaspar de Guzmán, Francisco de Quevedo wrote, at the beginning of the seventeeth century:

Pudo acusar los celos desiguales
a la Italia; pero hoy de muchos modos
somos copias, si son originales

(Italy he could blame of wavering faith;
but we in many fashions are today
mere copies: the originals are they).

For the Italian poetry of the Renaissance was not exclusively made of "Petrarchan stuff." It was also anti-Petrarchist, satirical, realistic, epic, and at its best highly personal.

III

Anti-Petrarchism was the reaction to that poetry which knew how to capture the secrets of Petrarch's musical grace but not his soul. Like all literary reactions, it was both logical and illogical; logical, in that it marked the beginning of an inevitable spiritual rebellion; and also illogical, in that it remained, while counteracting the Petrarchist canon, within the very sphere of Petrarchism. Also, like all literary reactions, it was both consequential and concomitant. Francesco Berni, the most vehement anti-Petrarchist, did not start his relentless war when the Petrarchist legion had exhausted all its weapons, but in the midst of its onrushing fury. Similarly, not after but during the *Dolce Stil Nuovo* had the dissenting voice of an Angiolieri been heard in all its raucous cynicism.

With Francesco Berni started officially the "new" literary trend, the aim of which was realism. (Unofficially, Burchiello and Lasca and, in part, Lorenzo and Politian should also be considered.) But realism seemed so hopelessly far, and so deeply crushed beneath the golden weight of the "Petrarchan stuff," that it could only be approached and liberated through the drastic presentation of reality at its worst. Thus the most unpoetic and even sordid details of life were sought out and laid bare to man's sight. And when, for the sake of parody, those details were heavily exaggerated, anti-Petrarchism enslaved itself to its own vulgarity. Women's lice replaced the shining golden hair, and venereal diseases supplanted the innocuous languorousness of the smarting heart.

The poet's true liberation, then, was neither in the sweet appeasement of Petrarchism nor in the bitter violence of its caricature. His salvation was in his own inner world—in a moment of deep sincerity or of genuine human suffering felicitously revealed. Thus one may call "anti-Petrarchist" not only Francesco Berni but also Della Casa, Di Tarsia, Stampa, Colonna, Bembo, and Michelangelo at their best, that is, in the most exalted flashing of their poetic inspiration.

Certain themes recur frequently in Renaissance verse. Love, repentance, time, old age, death, and heaven, are, one may say, the Horatian "notum." One is now eager to see how this "notum" becomes "novum" in the liberating art of this or that poet. With this in mind, we may discover much that is valid in the deluge of the Renaissance *canzonieri*. In the case of Barbara Torelli, for instance, one sonnet, though linked to the old imagery of Cupid's darts, redeems itself at once into genuine feeling magnificently expressed. Similarly, Giovanni Della Casa finds his point of departure in Petrarch, yet his sonnet, "To a Forest," is a cry of deep, personal anguish. Gaspara Stampa, too, is initially a Petrarchist, but her feminine world is her own and in it she transforms the Petrarchism of her education. How such transmutation occurred through genuineness of poetic inspiration can be illustrated by an analysis of Michelangelo's poetry. Michelangelo was not a Petrarchist by temperament or even literary education, but only, so to speak, by accident. This is to say that, when in moments of merely literary or derivative inspiration he was tempted to play the Petrarchist, the rough and twisted and awkward masculinity of the form he chose (the only diction of which he was capable) contrasted harshly with the particular theme that had been chosen for him, and thus resulted in a diction which was typically baroque. But when, in moments of unliterary or true inspiration, his own life dictated the theme and his own temperament prompted the phrase, in spite of any baroque slant still evident and perhaps unavoidable, his poetry was new and his art unique. He was then himself as all true poets are.

And in a different way Ariosto and Folengo were too deeply involved in their own dreams to be even aware of Petrarchism. Not that the poet of *Orlando Furioso* did not pay his homage to both Petrarch and Plato in a number of sonnets, songs, and madrigals. But his important contribution to the poetry of the Renaissance (and we are not touching upon the two major works of the sixteenth century, *Orlando Furioso* and *Gerusalemme Liberata*) is in his *Satires*. His satirical vein, at times too local to be universally mordant, and too comically autobiographical to rise above the limits of its own characterization, is, however, a refreshing rill in the valley of Petrarchism, and belongs at its worst with Berni's *Capitoli* and at its best with Horace.

Teofilo Folengo detached himself completely from the Petrarchist world and its values. To wage his war on poets who filled their *canzonieri* with "mille fusaras," or infinite nonsense, and on literati who wasted their lives debating on the superiority of Latin over the vulgar tongue, he created his own language and his own fatherland. His language, which he called "macaronic," was a mixture of Latin, Florentine, Lombard, and even Neapolitan. His fatherland was a colossal, sonorous pumpkin, not of this world, where three thousand magical barber-dentists had the task of uprooting with their ruthless pincers as many poets' teeth as were the lies in their poems. His "macaronic" idiom was, unfortunately, too specialized to reach the uneducated, but his world was original and marvelously pre-Cervantesque.

Whether we speak of Petrarchism or anti-Petrarchism, the Renaissance was an epoch of poetry, and poetry was an awesome name revered by popes and respected by tyrants. In one of the sonnets which he wrote in prison and addressed to Giuliano de' Medici, Machiavelli pleaded for his freedom not in the name of justice and innocence but of poetry:

> *I wear, Giuliano, chains instead of shoes,*
> *and round my shoulders goes a rope six times;*
> *but I won't tell you all my other woes*
> *since thus are treated those who deal with rhymes.*

IV

It would be difficult to reduce to a few fundamental notes the entire poetic production of the Renaissance. Carried away by his own taste (and literary taste is never infallible), an anthologist, while giving perhaps more importance to one particular theme, has to admit that others would undoubtedly seem as important, had his choice taken a different turn. But in this case it is not too hazardous to say that four are the main and most significant "tempi" of this sustained symphony—love, death, time, and exile.

Love is, of course, the archer god that wounded Petrarch, but also a sneering demon stalking the lover on mountains and through deserts. It is the phoenix and the salamander, but also a golden chisel that carves the soul. It is promise of paradise, but also wickedness that uses and abuses the heart of an inexperienced young woman. It is desire for eternal perfection, but also heart-rending plea for the tangible token of a letter. It is innocuous word and deep thought, mere literature and true poetic feeling.

Death is the "uncertain pass," the transformation of the beloved into a star, the end of suffering, the tender blossom plucked by a merciless hand or cut by the passing plow, the unexpected thief or the long-invoked liberator; but it is also a hammer snatched from the uplifted arm of a smith, and an audacious lesson to the angels on the secret of carving a beautiful woman's face for the continuation of beauty on earth.

Time is the inclement transience of day and night, of winter and spring, but also the gift of care-charming sleep. It is the power that crushes arches and temples, but also the might that annuls the suffering of the heart. It is resignation to wounds and wrinkles, but it is also Icarus' flight.

And there is, too, the note of political exile, which, in an era of disorder and bloodshed, means vision of unity and desire for peace.

But these leit-motifs are not the entire symphony. One must listen attentively to each chord and to each dissonance to capture, if not the realization, the suggestion of other minor, or even major, melodies. For when all inspiration seems exhausted, and every note is only musical ornamentation, one suddenly hears in the poetry of Torquato Tasso a magnificent singing voice which alone makes the program impressive. In Tasso's *Aminta* Sannazaro's pastoral *Arcadia* becomes a world of rarefied beauty, an atmosphere of unsurpassed poetic innocence. In his *Rime*, on the other hand, along with remnants of Petrarchism touched and revitalized by a great genius, throbs the poetry inspired by the most unhappy life and, above all, the torment of a soul caught between Renaissance and Baroque. And finally one hears the two voices of Bruno and Campanella, more intellectual than lyrical, more philosophical than emotive, and perhaps already baroque in their accent. While in Bruno's poems the last Petrarchan echo is already so faint as to be hardly recognized, in Campanella's sonnets all Petrarchism is dead. His sonnet, "Of Himself," with which this Anthology ends, may at first seem linked to Petrarch and Bembo, yet there is nothing derivative in it. It is the autobiography of a man who spent most of his life in prison. The world of Laura is now a far, misty region, and appears almost irrelevant, so different is now man's cry, so real his anguish.

V

A cursory glance through the pages of this book will at once reveal the forms, or molds, most beloved of our Renaissance poets—the sonnet, the canzone, the madrigal, and the capìtolo.

The sonnet was originally an entangled metrical experiment with some of the poets of the Frederician "Scuola Siciliana" until Dante gave it an ethereal suppleness in which the spirit was able to express its longings fully and limpidly. But it was Petrarch who made it live by crystallizing its fluid levity and brittle essence. He found in the sonnet the most convenient and rapid medium for the expression of his moods, but he also knew how to conjoin immediacy of feeling with elegance of diction still within the structure of the fourteen-line composition. Those who merely look at Petrarch's rhymes will notice at once how unique they are for variety of consonantic and vocalic nature and for liquidity of sound; so much so that it is today a nearly impossible task to find in the mine of the rhyme-rich Italian language a word left unearthed and unused by the most musical poet of Italy. Thus the sonnet became Petrarch's exclusive realm to which only those poets were to find access who had a new idea to contribute, not a lesser sound to add. These poets are Della Casa, Di Tarsia, Stampa, Michelangelo, Tasso, Bruno, and Campanella, in their most fervid sincerity of inspiration and utmost felicity of diction. Consequently, the history of man's love became, after Petrarch, love of man's history on earth—a history, that is, of his bafflement before the force of time; of his doubt in the midst of the amorous passion; of surrender and despair in the knowledge of an unsatisfying human love; of roughness and massiveness of thought rebellious to any form or dress; of tormenting hesitation between sin and grace; of magnificent though perilous challenge to mankind's old beliefs, and, finally, of imprisonment and triumph. Through the Renaissance sonnet the attentive reader will be able to observe three centuries of Italian history, from the corruption of the Church in Avignon to the most unfortunate rigor of the Counter-Reformation.

Unlike the sonnet, the canzone made no outstanding progress during the Renaissance. It remained as Petrarch left it, passionate and mournful, political and even religious, but highly personal. Throughout the history of Italian literature, with the exception of Guinizelli's "Al Cor Gentil" and Cavalcanti's "Donna Mi Prega," the canzone is the exclusive province of three supreme poets—Dante, Petrarch, and Leopardi. Yet from the majesty of its concept springs the title of most of the poetic collections of the Renaissance, "canzoniere" meaning thus more "canto" in general than "canzone" in particular. (Detaching itself altogether from its Renaissance spirit, the word has in contemporary Italian become synonymous with song-book.) Neither Bernardo Tasso nor Annibal Caro is powerful and intimate enough to make us forget the enchantment of Dante's, and Petrarch's, canzone. Torquato Tasso's "To the Metaurus" is the only plausible link between the past and the future of the canzone, that is between the world of Laura and that of Leopardi's Sylvia.

But the madrigal moved nimbly and gracefully in the Renaissance atmosphere. It more or less retained the soul of Petrarch's "Young wondrous angel on her pinions borne," but it also developed a sophisticated penchant for the conceit, unknown to a poet whose resources of creativity did not depend on merely intellectual subtleties. The madrigal can take what the sonnet and the canzone cannot. It can live on charm or cleverness alone if charm and cleverness are clothed in agile music or fluid rhythm. Though it remained within the boundaries of Cupid's world, it tried, and at times was able, to adorn with new notes the theme of man's ancient smart. Boiardo, Bembo, Guidiccioni, and Alamanni are perhaps at their best when they entrust their lyrical moods to the short melody of the madrigal. To this Michelangelo added the sudden strength of a marmoreal conclusion—a couplet that undoubtedly prefigures the finality of the Shakespearean sonnet. In the second half of the sixteenth century Guarini and Tasso restored the madrigal to its pristine purity of sound and handed it to the musical genius of Monteverdi. Five years before Tasso's death, Thomas Watson published in England, "cum Priuilegio Regiae Maiestatis," his *Superius*, or "The First Sett of Italian Madrigalls Englished not to the sense of the original dittie, but after the affection of the Noate." On its cover appeared these other words, "There are also heere inserted two excellent Madrigalls of Master William Byrds, composed after the Italian vaine, at the request of the sayd Thomas Watson." This Italian vein of the madrigal in England was unquestionably a fruit of the Italian Renaissance.

The "capitolo" had, on the other hand, a vein wholly its own. Rather than Italian, it started and remained regional, and even provincial, in its development. Too colloquial in tone and too repetitious in color, it retained the dynamic pleasantness of its master but, like its master, it failed to recognize and avoid superficiality. Berni, in fact, is brilliant and yet monochromatic, in love with details and yet with little awareness of what is dispensable or indispensable. If considered a means rather than an artistic end, the capitolo will perhaps be fully appreciated for its salutary effects on Michelangelo, who, acclaimed by Berni, felt that his unprofessional verse had, after all, won a competent defender. Even Ariosto's *Satires*, which are in the spirit of Berni's *Capitoli*, fail to make of the new *genre* an international literary achievement. Their references are too local and personal, and their intimate music has no reverberation in its listeners. Perhaps the major contribution of the "capitolo" lies in that it proved through the exteriority of its rhyme pattern the only fragile link of the Renaissance with Dante's *Comedy*. But as the canzone belongs to three supreme singers, so is the labyrinth of the terza rima familiar only to two poets—Dante its inventor, and Monti its modern reviver.

VI

Once the criterion of omitting all lengthly poems has been adopted, it is inevitable that those poets should particularly suffer whose reputation is based on such poems alone. For this reason, Pulci, Boiardo, Ariosto, and Tasso, though represented with passages from their less significant works, suffer some kind of *diminutio capitis*. But such are the risks of all poetic "floreta."

At this point a word should be said about the device of translation which I have adopted, and of which the reader will, I hope, be readily aware. I have tried to be as faithful as possible to the original texts while keeping the variety of their meters. Seldom have I, for the sake of a rhyme or rhyme pattern, sacrificed or even disguised the poignancy of an idea or the poetic allusion of an adjective. In the case of Petrarch, for instance, I had to choose between a translation that looked like a sonnet and a sonnet that did not look like a translation. I chose the latter in the belief that true poetry does not need, so to speak, the crutches of the rhyme to walk in beauty through the ages. However, since the rhyme, when unavoidable and unexpected, can be responsible for the incantation and memorability of a particular line or strophe, in several instances I have kept some suggestion of it either through some rhymes sparingly used but not necessarily recurring as in the original poem, or through some assonances directly or indirectly conveying a feeling of the pristine ornament. What I have always kept is the original meter of all the poems translated, with the sole exception of one of Bembo's sonnets in which I was forced to alter the rhythm of the hendecasyllabic line so as to retain the least shade or overtone, the loss of which would have made Berni's parody of the same sonnet look quite unjust or heavily exaggerated.

The biographical sketches, which are only intended to give some quick information especially on poets perhaps totally unfamiliar to the reader, are based on the following sources: *Enciclopedia Treccani; Manuale della Letteratura Italiana* by A. D'Ancona and O. Bacci; *Pian dei Giullari* by P. Bargellini; *Scrittori Italiani* by P. Carli and A. Sainati; *Crestomazia Italiana* by G. Lipparini; the *Oxford Book of Italian Verse;* the Vallardi *Storia Letteraria d'Italia,* and E. H. Wilkins' *History of Italian Literature.*

To facilitate all possible reference to the Italian texts I have placed in the Table of Contents, after each title, the first line of the corresponding Italian poem. This device I deemed necessary inasmuch as in a few instances the first lines of some English poems do not coincide, for reasons of grammatical construction or aesthetic aim, with those of their originals.

These are, then, the Italian poets of the Renaissance—some of them great, and some small; some sweet, some bitter; some conventional, and some unconventional and already close to our modern idiom. Superficiality and depth, corruption of customs and sincerity of religious faith, cynicism and love, fashionable despair and intimate anguish, darkness and light—these are the things that follow or precede one another in the sole order of which the life of man's passions is capable. For the Italian Renaissance, more than the motivation of a similar rebirth in England, France, and Spain, was, above all, a new significant chapter in the history of mankind.

JOSEPH TUSIANI

College of Mount Saint Vincent, New York

ITALIAN POETS OF THE
RENAISSANCE

THE POETS

Francesco Petrarca (1304-1374)

Petrarch is the first exponent of that new unrest of man's spirit which Dante's genius had envisioned and felt in the creation of his Ulysses. His fame no longer rests on the sonorous hexameters of his *De Africa* or on the magnificent erudition scintillating through the pages of his minor Latin writings. To the world he is the poet of Laura as Dante is the singer of Beatrice.

Born in Arezzo, Petrarch studied law at Montpellier and Bologna. In Avignon, where he took the minor orders, thus starting an ecclesiastic career that was to assure him a stipend and facilitate his intellectual pursuit, he met Laura in 1326. He traveled extensively for pleasure and business. In 1341 the Roman Senate made him a poet laureate for his *De Africa*, which deals with the end of the first Punic war. Through his various diplomatic missions he remained a poet, literature being to him the one world he really understood and fully loved. Handsome, admired by women, respected by popes and kings, revered by men of letters, the tender father of two illegitimate children, keenly aware of his own talents, superlatively fastidious in everything he wrote, in love with Vergil and Saint Augustine, torn between Christian faith and pagan culture, Petrarch is all in his *Canzoniere*.

Handled by its supreme master, the Italian sonnet reached its insuperable perfection and became the most appropriate vehicle of expression for the poet's complex and fluctuating moods or spiritual states. It is supple, terse, colorful, melodious, and therefore almost untranslatable in its nuances. What remains, in the case of this poet, is perhaps the nucleus of his artistic sincerity. All the other components, such as the tenderness of a diminutive, the sound of a double consonant, or the elegance of a rhyme, are sacrificed to the immediate exigencies of the foreign idiom.

IT WAS THE DAY THE SUN GREW
PALE AND LOW

It was the day the sun grew pale and low
in doleful deference to its Maker's last,
when, all-unguarded, lady, I was fast
bound with your glances' unexpected glow.
'Twas not the time to fear Love's nearing blow,
it seemed to me; safe and without the least
doubt, on my way I went: thus my unrest
began together with the whole world's woe.

Love found and caught me utterly unarmed,
seeing the entrance open to my heart
through these my eyes, now door to all my tears.
Therefore it was no honor, it appears,
to wound me at that moment with his dart,
and hide his bow from you, so fully armed.

LOOSE IN THE BREEZE, THE GOLD
OF ALL HER HAIR

Loose in the breeze, the gold of all her hair
was in a thousand playful ringlets blown,
and more than ever the great luster shone
of those fair eyes, less ardent now and fair.
And (was I right or wrong?) a hue was there,
a gleam of mercy until then unknown:
I who had tinder in my breast, not stone,
what wonder I was kindled unaware?

Her bearing was no mortal happening
but an angelic grace, and all her words
did not as simply human voices ring.
A sun, a spirit from the firmament
was the new life I saw, and, were it not,
no wound is healing though the bow relent.

4

AWAY THE DEAR OLD MAN WHITE-HAIRED
AND PALE

Away the dear old man, white-haired and pale,
goes from the place where all his age was spent,
and from his little loving family
that see, in terror, their own father fail.
Dragging from there his ancient body on
through the remaining daylight of his life,
he walks and walks, borne by his will alone,
despite his years and all distress and strife—

and comes to Rome, where he fulfills his wish
of gazing at the image of the One
he hopes once more in Paradise to view.
So I, alas, my lady, often go
seeking, as far as possible, in others
the true and longed-for beauty that is you.

PENSIVE, ALONE, EACH MOST
ABANDONED FIELD

Pensive, alone, each most abandoned field
with slow and tardy step I pace and pace,
my glances bent and quick no more to face
a human imprint on the sand revealed.
No other way have I, no other shield
against those people who can surely trace,
in all my deeds no more with joy ablaze,
the fire whereby my heart is seared and sealed.

Thus every shore and mountain, I believe,
and every wood and river know what kind
of life I lead, though hidden from mankind.
Yet of no savage path can I conceive,
or one so harsh, where Love would not come by,
talking with me, and waiting my reply.

WHEN RAPIDLY THE SUN SEEMS TO DECLINE

When rapidly the sun seems to decline
toward west, and this our day flies to the other
side of the earth where men await its light,
seeing herself in a far land, alone,
the weary weak old woman on the road
quickens her step, and hastens more and more;
and lonesome though she be,
now that her day is ended,
she does some solace find
in her brief rest whereby she can forget
the ill and boredom of the trodden miles.
But, oh, the grief that in the day I bore
increases in my heart
when the eternal light's with us no more.

As soon as the sun turns its flaming wheels
to let night pass, whereat down from the highest
mountains a greater shadow quick descends,
the frugal hoeman gathers all his tools
and, singing then an alpine song or tune,
clears of all sadness his encumbered breast;
he fills his table then
with food as poor as those
old acorns which this world
has often praised but still disdains to touch.
Oh, let all those who care, at times be gay!
But, as for me, this only news is true:
no joy or even rest,
though sky or planet turn, I ever knew.

The hour the lofty planet's rays are seen
to set into the nest that harbors them,
the shepherd, seeing all the east grow dim,
rises and, staff in hand, tenderly moves
his whole flock onward, leaving grass and fountains
and leafy beeches in much haste behind;

far from all people then,
he strews with verdant leaves
his little hut or den,
and, carefree and at ease, lies down to sleep.
But, cruel Love, upon that very time
you force me all the more to seek and find
a woman's voice or step—
one you have taught the motions of a hind.

And in some tranquil bay the seamen rest,
now that the sun has set, their worn-out limbs
under rough blankets on a wooden plank.
But, though its light has plunged into the sea,
leaving behind Granada, Spain, and far
Morocco and the Pillars;
though men and women, and
each animal and land
now rest from grief and ache,
I cannot yet relieve my restless pain,
and blame the day for my far worsened smart.
Ah, with this ever-growing, great desire
ten years I now have lived,
and do not know who'll free me from such fire.

And, since I vent my anguish with my words,
I see at evening loosened oxen come
back from the fields and from the furrowed hills:
but when shall I be ridden of my sighs?
when will this heavy burden leave my life?
and why am I still weeping, day and night?
What did I wish to gain
when first I fixed my gaze
upon that winsome face
so that I might engrave it with my thought
here in my heart, whence neither force nor art
will ever cancel it, till it be prey
to Death, who sunders all?
And of this, too, I know not what to say.

My Song, if being here
from morning unto night
has made you one with me,
you must not long to show yourself elsewhere.
For others' praises little will you care,
for it will be enough from hill to hill
to think how this live stone,
on which I lean, has burned my wish and will.

MADRIGAL

Young wondrous angel on her pinions borne
came down from heaven on the dewy bank
where I was passing ('twas my fate) alone.

Seeing me unescorted, unafraid,
a net that she had woven out of silk
right in the greenness of my path she laid.

So I was caught, and did not seem to mind,
so kindling were her glances, and so kind.

FATHER OF HEAVEN, AFTER LOSS OF DAYS

Father of Heaven, after loss of days,
and after nights in futile struggle spent
with that harsh longing that my spirit rent,
recalling deeds so fair for my disgrace,
may You now grant that with your light I face
a nobler life, a more divine ascent,
so that my bitter enemy, intent
on catching me, I soon away may chase.

Now the eleventh year, my Lord, is turning
since I was bent beneath the ruthless yoke,
fiercer upon those souls that more are burning.
Have mercy on so base an anguish; guide
my erring thoughts to better havens: tell them
on such a day you once were crucified.

COOL, LIMPID, LOVELY STREAM

Cool, limpid, lovely stream,
where she her beauty bathed,
who does to me the only lady seem!
O gentle bough (remembering is sighing)
which she so fondly loved
as to appear so fair against it lying!
O grass and blossoms that her graceful gown
rendered so sweet with her angelic breast
when gently she sat down!
Air, luminous and blest,
where Love unlocked my heart with her fair glance:
may all of you now give
heed to these last imploring words that grieve.

It it is still my fate
 (and Heaven makes it true)
that Love should close these eyes while still they weep,
may some sweet grace my buried body keep
here, amongst all of you,
while, naked, my soul seeks its first abode.
Death will less cruel be
if with this hope I go
on that uncertain road:
for never could my weary spirit leave
its anguished flesh and bones
in a more tranquil haven or find rest
for my poor ashes in a tomb more blest.

Perhaps a day will rise
when my so fair and fierce beloved may
come to her well known place;
and here, where first she saw
me standing on that first and blessèd day,
maybe she'll turn her glad, inquiring gaze,
looking for me; but, oh,
finding not me but only earth and stone,

Love will perhaps inspire her, and obtain
her gentle sigh and moan
whereby she will implore God's grace for me,
and on the Sky prevail,
drying her eyelids with her charming veil.

Down from the beauteous boughs
(so sweet 'tis to recall)
a rain of buds into her lap descended,
and humble there, and splendid,
she sat in so much glory,
covered at once by all that loving shower.
One flower upon her hem,
and still another flower
fell on her tresses glistening and gay,
which furbished gold and pearl
seemed to my eyes, that day;
one rested on the ground, and still another
fell on the flowing water;
another still, with restless roundelay,
"The realm of Love is here," appeared to say.

How many times did I
say then, in sudden fear,
"She was, for certain, born in Paradise!"
Her face, her words, her eyes,
her divine bearing, her entrancing smile,
had charged me with so much forgetfulness,
and so removed me from
reality of sight,
that, sighing, I could only whisper then,
"How did I come here? When?"—
deeming myself in Heav'n, not where I stood.
From that time forth, this grass
I have so loved, I find but here all peace.

If, O my Song, you had your longed-for glow,
boldly at once you could
fare among men outside this lonely wood.

11

FROM THOUGHT TO THOUGHT

From thought to thought, from mountain on to mountain,
Love leads me still, for every trodden way
proves hostile to tranquillity of life.
If on some lonely shore springs rill or fountain,
if a dark dell between two hillocks lies,
there my bewildered spirit finds some peace;
and, heeding Love's advice,
it laughs, or weeps, or fears, or hopes again;
and there my face that with my spirit goes
is clouded, and then glows,
and long in the one state does not remain;
so that an expert of such things would swear,
looking at me, "He burns, quite unaware."

In the high mountains, in wild woods I find
my solace; every place where people dwell
is to my sight a mortal enemy.
With every step I take a thought is born
of my sweet lady, which can often turn
the anguish that she causes into bliss.
No sooner would I yearn
to change the bittersweet ways of my life,
than I reflect, "Love has for you—who knows—
a better time in store;
someone perhaps loves you, who loathe yourself so much."
And in this thought I am still sighing then:
Could such a thing be true? But how? or when?

Where a tall pine tree or a hill gives shade
I often pause, yet on the nearest stone
I limn her lovely features with my mind.
When to my senses I return, I find
tears streaming on my chest, and sadly moan:
"What have you come to! And how far you are!"
But while in that first thought
I can take hold of my fast-wandering mind,
and see her still, and all of me forget,

I, then, feel Love so near
that my soul loves its own meandering:
so fair I see her, in so many a place,
that, should illusion last, it would be grace.

Many a time (will you believe me now?)
I've seen her present in a limpid stream,
and on the verdant grass, and in the bark
of beechen trees, and in white clouds, so fair
that Leda would have thought her daughter dim
as is a star the sun hides in his ray.
The lonelier the shore,
and the more wild the place where I may be,
the fairer to my thought she seems to be.
Then, when reality
chases the sweet illusion, there I sit,
cold, a dead stone upon a living stone,
like one who thinks and weeps and writes alone.

Up to the highest and most barren peak,
untouched by shadow of some other mountain,
a piercing longing ever bids me go.
There I begin to measure with my glance
all of my woes and, weeping, thus I vent
the anguish that like mist o'erfloods my heart,
when, looking down, I brood
on all the winds that keep me far apart
from that fair face, ever so near yet far.
Soft to myself I say,
"Why grieve, poor soul, so much? Perhaps down there,
moaning how far you are, she sighs for you!"
And in this thought my soul can breathe anew.

My song, beyond those alps,
there, where the sky shines clearer and more gay,
once more you'll see me near a flowing brook,
there where the air smells sweet
with the fresh fragrance of a Laurel tree.
There dwells the one who stole my heart from me;
here you may gaze on my sole effigy.

13

PEACE I HAVE NOT, AND STILL NO BATTLE FIGHT

Peace I have not, and still no battle fight;
I fear and hope; I am aflame and freeze;
on clouds I fly and sit among the trees;
nothing I grasp and hold the whole world tight.
The one who shut all freedom from my sight
calls me not hers, yet keeps me ever bound;
Love does not kill me, but heals not my wound,
and wants me dead, yet bids me live in fright.

No eyes have I, and see; no tongue, and shout;
I long to die, and succor I await;
myself I loathe but someone else I love.
Weeping, I laugh; with woe my days I sate,
and death and life displease me equally:
lady, for you am I in such a state.

OH, WHERE IN HEAVEN, IN WHAT GODLY THOUGHT

Oh, where in heaven, in what godly thought
was once the mold whence Nature, long ago,
learnt this fair face whereby she deigned to show
to us poor mortals what on high is wrought?
What nymph in forest or in rill was caught
giving the breeze such hair of golden glow?
When in one heart did so much virtue grow?
(Ah, life to me such lavishness has not!)

In vain for divine beauty will one sigh
who never saw this wondrous woman's eyes
as gently she can turn them, passing by.
He will not know how love can heal and slay,
who never saw with what rare charm she sighs,
and sweetly speaks and smiles along her way.

BOTH LOVE AND I, SO DAZED WITH WONDERMENT

Both Love and I, so dazed with wonderment
as those appear who ne'er such bliss could see,
gaze at the one whose talk or smile can be,
oh, never to another lady lent.
From her fair glances' limpid firmament
so do those two firm stars shine bright to me,
no better guide can set a pilgrim free
or kindle one on love's best height intent.

O rarest wonder when she's seen to rest—
herself a blossom—in the blooming grass,
or press a verdant bush with her white breast!
How sweet, at dawn of spring, is to behold
this lady, unescorted, pensive, pass,
weaving a wreath around her curls of gold!

NOW WHILE THE SKY, THE EARTH, THE WIND ARE STILL

Now while the sky, the earth, the wind are still,
and bird and beast by taming sleep are bound;
while the night leads its starry car around,
and the sea lies with neither waves nor will;
I wake and weep, and brood and burn, the one
who so unmakes me ever on my mind:
by grief and anger I am fought and won,
yet if I think of her my peace I find.

So from the same clear, lively fountain both
the sweet and bitter start on which I feed;
one single hand both heals and makes me bleed.
And so that this my ache may reach no shore,
a thousand times I'm born and die each day,
my sole salvation far forevermore.

WITH BUT ONE FONDLING THOUGHT THAT MAKES ME BE

With but one fondling thought that makes me be
away from men, and fare through life alone,
at times I sunder my own self from me,
seeking her still, whom I should only shun.
So cruel and so kind I see her run,
my spirit trembles with desire to flee,
such are the full-armed sighs with which I'm won
by this fair enemy of Love and me.

A ray of truth, if I am right to say,
truly I glimpse on that proud clouded brow,
which somehow brightens my deep-grieving heart.
I summon up my soul then, and as I
decide to bare my ill intent, so much
have I to tell her that I dare not start.

BEAUTIFUL HAND, THAT HOLD MY HEART SO TIGHT

Beautiful hand, that hold my heart so tight,
and keep my life in such a narrow space!
Nature and God, to show their worth and grace,
lavished on you all of their art and light.
Five Eastern pearls you are, oh, far more bright,
O soft, dear fingers, harsh upon my wound,
yet now, to make me dream of rich delight,
by Love laid bare before me for a while.

O smooth, white glove that I so dearly touch,
and once concealed fresh roses of bright dawn:
was ever trophy in this world so sweet?
Would that of her fair veil I saw as much!
O human things, most changeable and fleet!
But what I stole no longer must I own.

O LITTLE ROOM, ONCE HARBOR
OF DELIGHT

O little room, once harbor of delight
against my grievous tempests and my fears,
and now a fountain of nocturnal tears
which back, within the day, for shame I fight!
O little bed, once comfort in my plight
and endless woe, from what distressing urns
Love bathes you now with those fair ivory hands
that, so unjustly, but to me give fright!

Oh, not away from rest and troth I go,
but more from my own self and my own mind,
which, heeded, raised me often to the sky.
And in the crowd, my once detested foe,
(who would have thought it?) now my port I find,
such fear of being still alone have I.

WHAT ARE YOU DOING NOW? WHAT ARE
YOU THINKING?

What are you doing now? What are you thinking?
Why look behind to what can be no more,
O weary soul of mine? Why to the fire
in which you burn are you new wood still bringing?
The winsome words, the looks of lively cheer
you have described and painted in their glow
have from this world been snatched, and well you know
'tis late and early both to seek them here.

The thing that kills us, ah, do not renew,
but, casting every false vain hope away,
find in firm faith your only saving way.
Heaven let's seek if naught can please on earth:
on her fair face we wrongly fixed our view
if, live and dead, it led our peace astray.

17

WHAT SHALL I DO? WHAT DO YOU, LOVE, SUGGEST?

What shall I do? What do you, Love, suggest?
This is the time to die;
and I have tarried more than I should wish.
My lady's dead, and took my heart along.
Now, if I claim it back,
these sinful years I only have to break,
for I no longer hope
to see her here, and waiting is distress.
My every happiness,
since she has fled, has turned into dismay,
and my life's sweetness is all gone away.

O Love, you know ('tis you, therefore, I blame)
how harsh and grievous all my losses are;
and I know, too, you pity me my woes,
our woes, for our ship crashed
against one cliff, our sun
at the same time turned dark.
What mind could now relate
merely with words the anguish of my state?
Ah, thankless world bereaved!
You have all reasons to lament with me,
for with her death you've lost
the only good of which you once did boast.

Your glory's fallen, and you see it not;
nor were you worthy, while
on earth she dwelt, to know her
or to be trodden by her holy feet,
because so fair a thing
was destined to adorn
with its own life the firmament above.
But I, who now, alas, without her, love
neither myself nor mortal life, in tears
forever call her back:
of so much hope but this is left to me,
and this alone can force me here to be.

O woe! mere dust is now her beauteous face,
which used to prove down here
heaven and its supernal happiness:
her form unseen is now in paradise,
rid of that veil at last
which cast a shadow on her age's bloom,
and which she will resume
once more, never to leave it, when, one day,
her we shall see, so much
more fair and bright as lasting beauty's worth
cannot compare with mortal one on earth.

A lady far more beautiful and kind,
oh, she appears to me,
there, where she knows her sight is welcome most.
This of my life is now the one support,
the other is her clear
name that so sweetly murmurs in my heart:
but as I recollect
how dead my hope is now, which was alive
while she was blooming here,
Love sees what I become, and she, too, knows
(I hope), who to God's truth is now so close.

O ladies, you who on her beauty gazed
and the angelic life
with that celestial bearing on this earth,
for me be sorry and by pity moved,
and not for her, who soared
to so much peace, and in such war left me
that, since now fate far more
impedes my step to follow her, I quick
would break this knot: but Love
soon halts my hand with what he has to say,
for, deep within, he reasons in this way:

"Ah, check this anguish leading you astray,
for by excessive wish
you may lose heaven, which your heart so craves,
and where lives she who seems to others dead,
and softly smiles at what
was her fair spoil, and sighs for you alone,
and begs you not to let
her fame, which you have spread
into so many lands, now quickly die:
but make her name's renown ever more clear,
if her fair eyes to you were truly dear."

Keep from the green away
and from bright skies; go not near joy or laughter,
my Song, oh no, but stay where dwells distress:
among glad people you must not be seen,
widow disconsolate in a black dress.

IF BIRD IN MOURNFULNESS, OR VERDANT LEAF

If bird in mournfulness, or verdant leaf
in blandness moving to the summer breeze,
or raucous murmur of clear waves that pleas
I hear from some fresh bank in bloom; and if
I'm writing there of love and my belief,
'tis her, whom Heaven showed and earth does seize,
I see and hear and answer, as I please,
replying from afar to all my grief.

"Why waste your life, before your time, away,"
she tells me in her pity; "Why still pour
so many tears of infinite dismay?
Oh, weep for me no more: my day became,
through death, eternal, and, in closing them,
my eyes I opened to my inner flame."

THE EYES I SANG SO WARMLY OVER AGAIN

The eyes I sang so warmly over again,
and, ah, those arms and hands, those feet, that face,
which had so raised me from my truthful place,
and made me singular amongst all men;
that waving hair of pure and lucent gold,
and the bright flash of that angelic smile
which turned this earth to paradise meanwhile,
are now a handful of insentient mold.

And yet I live; at which myself I scorn,
having been left without that much loved light,
mid-ocean, on a ship by tempest torn.
Let my love song die too, no more in keeping:
dry is the vein of my once easy thought,
and this my lyre is now all turned to weeping.

O VALLEY, SO REPLETE WITH MY LAMENT

O valley, so replete with my lament;
river, that these my tears make overflow;
wild beasts, and winsome birds, and fish that grow
enclosed between two banks, green, redolent;
air, rendered by my sighing so content;
pathway, so bitter now but sweet before;
hill, so much cherished once and now no more,
which out of habit Love and I ascend:

her well-known forms I still can trace in you—
oh, not in me, who from so glad a life
have now become a harbor of distress.
From here my living joy I used to view—
now but a mound of earth where, flown to God,
her spirit left its mortal loveliness.

IT WAS MY MIND THAT TOOK ME TO THE PLACE

It was my mind that took me to the place
where dwells the one I cannot find below:
and there, in the third heaven's living glow,
I saw, more fair and less unkind, her face.
Taking me by the hand, "You'll also stay
up here," she said, "if all your longing's true:
I'm she who waged so wild a war on you,
and before evening ended my one day.

"To understand my bliss, your thoughts would fail:
for you alone I wait, and what you love
so much, and is on earth—my lovely veil."
Oh, why did she, at this, her hand remove?
For at those gentle words' most pitying sound
almost in Heaven I myself had found.

THAT NIGHTINGALE, SO TENDERLY IMPLORING

That nightingale, so tenderly imploring,
mourns a dear fledgling or beloved mate,
and skies and fields with sweetness seems to sate,
so many piercing, pitying notes outpouring.
Throughout the night that song, so sadly faring,
following me, reminds me of my fate:
myself I blame, who did not deem Death great
enough to win a goddess with his daring.

How easy to deceive a man's belief!
Those two fair lights, far brighter than the Sun,
who would have thought could turn into dark earth?
Well I know now, my ruthless destiny
wants me to learn through life and endless grief
how nothing here can last and joyful be.

I WEEP AND WEEP OVER MY SEASONS PAST

I weep and weep over my seasons past,
which I spent loving but a thing of earth,
with no more zest for flight, though I had wings
to give no base examples of my worth.
You, Who can see my wicked, impious ills,
invisible, immortal King of Heaven,
aid this my soul, so strayed and frail, and fill
with all your grace the chasm of its dearth:

so that, if I have lived in war and tempest,
I may in peace and in a harbor die;
and if my stay was vain, my going at least
be truthful. Toward this little of my life
still left, and in my death, oh, stretch your hand!
Full well You know in no one else I trust.

TO THE BLESSED VIRGIN

. . . .

Virgin, I have already wept so much,
so much entreated, so much begged in vain,
to my regret and grievous harm alone!
Since on the bank of Arno I was born,
seeking now one and now some other shore,
nothing but anguish this my life has been.
Beauty that dies, and words, and actions, have
sorely my soul oppressed.
O Virgin pure and blest,
hasten: I have perhaps reached my last year.
Much fleeter than a dart my days have fled
in misery and sin,
and Death alone is waiting now, instead.

Virgin, mere earth is she, and has much pained
my heart, who held it weeping while alive,
and of my thousand woes knew not a one,
and, had she known, would have prevented none
of all the things that passed: her different wish
would have been death to me; to her, ill fame.
Now you, Heavenly Lady, you, our Goddess
(if I might use such name),
Virgin of high acclaim,
you see all things; and what no man could do
your might can now most easily achieve:
bring to an end my plight—
a thing that, saving me, would honor you.

Virgin, in whom I place my every hope
that you will help me in my final need,
desert me not upon my final step.
Not me—remember Him who deigned to make me;
and not my worth—let His high image in me
spur you to mercy for so base a man.

Medusa and my own illusion turned me
into ill-dripping stone.
With tears devout and holy,
Virgin, oh, fill my sad and wearied heart:
so that at least my final weeping be
so rid of earthly mud
as my first one was not devoid of folly.

Virgin, O tender enemy of pride,
may fondness of our one Beginning move you.
Have pity on a contrite, humble heart:
for, if a bit of fleeting mortal dust
I'm wont to love with such uncommon trust,
how should I love you then—a gentle thing?
If from my wretched state of suffering,
thanks to your hand, I rise,
O Virgin, to your name
I'll consecrate pure thoughts and mind and style,
and lips and heart, and all my tears and sighs.
Show me the safest ford,
and, please, accept my new desires meanwhile.

The day is nearing and cannot be far,
such is time's race or flight,
O Virgin one and only,
and now remorse, now death, pricks this my heart.
Oh, recommend me to your Son, true Man,
true God, that in my death
He may receive in peace my final breath.

FROM *THE TRIUMPHS*

(I, 160-172)

Not as a flame put out by force of breeze,
but as one growing by itself less bright,
her happy spirit went away in peace.

Just as a tranquil and transparent light,
little by little losing wick and glow,
comes to the end of its allotted right,

oh no, not pale, but far more white than snow
windlessly falling on some lovely hill,
she seemed to rest like one too tired to go.

A sleep had come to seal her radiant eyes—
her soul already having left this place—
a gentle sleep called death by men unwise.

Death looked so lovely on her lovely face.

TO ITALY

My Italy, though words can never heal
the mortal wounds I see
so countless in your body, still so fair,
it pleases me my sighs at least can be
such as are hoped for still
by Tiber, Arno, and Po River where
I'm living in great sorrow and dismay.
Heavenly King, I pray:
for that sweet love that brought you on man's earth,
oh, turn to this beloved, kindly land!
See, gracious Lord, how from no cause at all
so fierce a war had birth!
You, Father, open, soften, and make free
the hearts that Mars is holding in his thrall,
and there now let your truth, despite my wrong,
be heard from this my tongue.

You, in whose hands Luck placed the bridle of
these regions of delight,
for which your hearts have shown no ruth or love:
why are so many alien swords still here?
So that this verdant earth
may soon be painted with barbaric blood?
A vain mistake, I fear,
deludes you: little you see, and still believe
you see too much, since you still look for faith
in mercenary souls.
He who most people owns
is most surrounded by his bitter foes.
Oh, what odd deluge flows
from far and foreign deserts on our fields!
If all this comes about by our own hands,
who will there be to save our pleasant lands?

Nature provided for our shelter well
when she devised the Alps
as shield between us and the German wrath.
But blind desire has blindly found a path
against itself, succeeding thus in bringing
sores to the lovely limbs.
Now, look, in the one cage,
wild beasts and docile flocks are forced to dwell,
so that the worse inflict their cruel rage:
and, to our greater grief, this is the seed
of that old, lawless throng
whose side was once laid open, as we read,
by Marius so cruelly, one day,
that we shall ne'er forget his dauntless deed,
when, thirsty, weak yet bold,
he drank not water from the stream, but blood.

Caesar I mention not, who, where he went,
incarnadined the grass
with blood that Latin arms drew from their veins.
It seems now, I know not by what ill stars,
that Heaven hates us all, oh, thanks to you
to whom so much was granted:
'tis your divided wills that now lay waste
this land, the world's most beautiful and splendid.
What guilt, what judgment, or what ill unrest
drives you to vex your lowly neighbor so,
and crave the remnants of his scattered wealth,
and call for foreign foe,
and then rejoice that still new blood be shed,
and life be cheaply sold at any price?
I but the truth relate,
and neither speak from men's contempt or hate.

After so many a proof, can you not see
how the Bavarians cheat,
who, raising but a finger, toy with death?
Shame, as I see it, worsens our defeat.
But your blood flows more lavishly because
of your new wrathful breath.
From matins unto terce
think of yourselves, and you will realize
how those who cherish others
only themselves despise.
O gentle Latin blood,
shake from yourself this harmful yoke at once:
do not idolatrize
a futile, empty name,
for, if the rage of Northern backward throngs
our intellect can win,
'tis not through Nature's fault but our own sin.

And is this not the ground that I first touched?
Is not this place the nest
where I was nurtured and so sweetly blest?
And is this not the native land in which
I place all of my trust—
the mother, sweet and kind,
who covers both my parents with her dust?
Oh, in God's name, let this
sometimes uplift the mind.
With great compassion look
upon the tears of all our men oppressed,
who, after God, of you alone beg rest.
For, if you show the least
glimmer of pity, then
will valor clash in war
against all wrath: the fighting shall be brief,
for ancient valor and its memory
are firing still the heart of Italy.

My Lords, behold how time is flying fast,
how this our life on earth
is running, and how death is at our back.
You are now here, but you are your own past,
for, naked and alone,
the soul must come to that uncertain pass.
So, while this vale you cross,
may you lay down both hatred and disdain,
winds that annul serenity of life.
The time you spend in causing others grief,
oh, turn into a new
and nobler deed of praise—
the action of your hand or of your thought
or some research that may reward all men:
thus can we know delight on earth, and find
open the road to Heaven for mankind.

Let me now warn you, Song:
explain your reasons courteously to all,
because among proud men you're now to go,
whose hearts and minds are full
of the worst kind of prejudice and hate—
truth's most relentless foe.
So take your chance among
the small, good-hearted throng
in love with what is good and honest. This
you'll say to them: I plead for peace, peace, peace.

Giovanni Boccaccio (1313-1375)

The author of the *Decameron* wrote more verse than prose. Without a teacher and against his father's wish, he studied and learned the Poetics. As in his major work, even in his verse, such as *Teseida, Filostrato, Caccia di Diana,* and *Rime,* one can trace Boccaccio's experience as a lover, a scholar, and a deeply religious man. He was not the jolly, unscrupulous, immoral or amoral humanist easily and hastily associated with some pages of his *Decameron.* His life, vexed in its last years by poverty and illness, and comforted by a profound, unfaltering faith in God, was thoroughly devoted to the cult of art and friendship. Incapable of envy, and aware of his own poetic limitations, he had two great enlightening loves in his youth and old age—Dante's *Comedy* and the poetry of Petrarch. To Dante he devoted his enthusiastic research, and Petrarch he called his dearest friend on earth. In Petrarch's will there is the touching detail of fifty gold florins bequeathed to Boccaccio so that he might buy a furred cloak for his nocturnal ambulations.

Boccaccio's poetry, which restlessly moves from the canzone to the sonnet, from the *ottava rima* to the ballad, does not always attain that power of synthesis and that economy of imagery which are expected of a poet. Though enamored of classical antiquity and aware of the *stil nuovo* tradition, he was tempted by the burlesque trend, and he interspersed his verse with it, not always succeeding in turning realism into flashing truth. But at times, as in the following sonnets, Boccaccio's verse can reach the limpidity of true emotion.

31

LOVE IN WINTER

Rivers have turned to glass, and rivulets
are blocked and frozen by cold winds that blow.
Plainlands and peaks are covered with white snow,
branches are barren, gone all flowerets.
Dead is the tender grass, and no birds sing,
this season being so hostile to their nature.
The bitter northwind roars, and every creature
is locked indoors, afraid and shivering.

I, I alone, for love still grieve and pine,
burning in such great flames that Vulcan's fire
is but a tiny spark compared to mine.
And day and night I lift my hands in prayer,
from my harsh lord some water to obtain,
but not one drop he sends on my despair.

BIRDS, THERE ARE BIRDS

Birds, there are birds enamored so of light
that, as they lie, after the day is ended,
deep in their nest, with one another blended,
if the least sound should stir, and a faint light
appear, they rise, and follow soon that bright
glimpse, once more eager to pursue their splendid
delight, full unaware they're being bended
by their false guide to traps of grief and fright.

The same thing happens, O my God, to me:
as soon as those two radiant, ruthless eyes
bid all my longings speed where'er she be,
I run at once, most eager and unwise,
myself in faster fetters then to see,
from which I had been hoping free to rise.

32

REVENGE

If it should happen I live long enough
to see her golden tresses turn all gray,
which make me, keep me so in love today,
and her smooth face become all wrinkled, rough,
her beauteous eyes, which at my sorrow laugh,
suddenly blear, her precious breasts hang dry,
and her soft-singing voice painfully die
into a raucous screech: how better off

will I be then! My sighs, my grief, my weeping
will turn to laughter, and I'll promptly say:
"Woman, you are no longer in Love's keeping,
no more to your sweet music am I prey:
so pale and wilted and so worthless, go,
and mourn your sterile pride of long ago."

THE CURSE OF BAIA

If Baia's sea and heaven I abhor,
its lakes and fountains, and its waves and sand,
the known and unknown corners of this land,
no one, indeed, should wonder any more.
With feasts of song and dancing on this shore,
and with a blab of ever-empty sound,
all hearts are taken and all minds are bound
where only feats of love come to the fore.

Venus is seen so freely here to roam
that, often, a Lucretia coming out
goes with the shame of Cleopatra home.
How well I know! I therefore have no doubt
that this corruption, so far-spread and true,
has won the spirit of my lady, too.

A LESSON

I do not dare lift up my gaze again
    a lovely girl to see,
when I recall what one has done to me.

No lover ever loved with such a heart
    or with such pure desire
as I loved once my lady, I confess.

But when, for all my loyalty and smart,
    I thought I'd earned her bliss,
one I did not suspect became her sire.

So now I bend my eyes and check my fire,
    saying, "All women shun,
for all perhaps are false like that first one."

A DIFFICULT CHOICE

Love often calls to my attention two
equally lovely ladies: one appears
as virtuous as she is fair and true;
the second somewhat wins the first in years.
They do not dress alike: a different hue
makes different the gown each woman wears,
because of which my ruling Lord, as you
will soon find out, still whispers in my ears:

"That charming girl that goes and truly beams
is a sweet virgin full of love and youth;
the other, clad in black, a widow seems.
Since, at one time, you cannot love them both,
I'll give you only one, not two together:
so tell me frankly which would suit you better."

Believe me, Love, this is the hardest question:
I therefore come to you for your suggestion.

CHEAPLY HAVE I ABUSED

Cheaply have I abused the Muses so
that to a brothel I have brought them all,
causing their most intimate parts to fall
beneath the stare of their plebeian foe.
But let no longer such offences go
against me, for Apollo with his gall
has on my flesh already avenged them all
so that no limb is free from his hard blow.

I was a man, and am a wineskin full,
oh, not of wind, but of most grievous lead,
so grievous I can hardly walk at all.
And will this boredom end? I know not how,
so one with it am I, from toe to head:
oh, only God, I hope, can help me now.

TO DANTE

Dante, if high within the sphere of love,
as I believe, you dwell, and gaze upon
your Bicè fair, who through your song before
had raised you where she had already gone;
if, rising from mendacious to true life,
one still remembers love, then I implore
you, in her name, to grant me what to you,
who see all this, is a small thing to do.

Among the souls in the third heaven blest
I know full well my Fiammetta sees
the grief that since her passing has been mine.
Beg her—if taste of Lethe's keen delight
still binds her to me—for this sign of love,
that I to her may presently take flight.

ON THE DEATH OF PETRARCH

Now you have climbed at last, O my dear lord,
to the sweet realm where those who God still know
are by His providence allowed to go
when they abandon this our wicked world.
Now you are there, where often your desire
to gaze on your Lauretta bade you rise—
there, where my lovely Fiammetta lies
beside her in God's marvelous empire.

Now with Sennuccio, Cino, and Dante, you
can live assured of your eternal rest,
looking on ecstasies I never knew.
Oh, if on this sad earth you cherished me,
take me where I may watch, forever blest,
the lady that with love first kindled me.

TO THE BLESSED MOTHER

No golden tress or loveliness of glance,
no regal bearing or entrancing face,
no youthfulness of age or song of mirth,
and no angelic mien or beauty's grace
could ever draw from all his sovereign height
the King of Heaven on this wicked earth,
and make him, Mary dear, in you have birth,
Mother of grace and mirror of delight.

'Twas your humility with all its might
broke the old rancor between us and God,
and bade the heavens open once again.
Lend us this virtue, Holy Mother, then,
so that, preceded by it, climb we may
to your blest kingdom piously one day.

Franco Sacchetti (1330?-1400)

Born probably at Ragusa, Franco Sacchetti went to Florence, it is believed, in 1362. There he participated in the political life of the city, becoming one of the most prominent personalities of that Commune. He held several posts until he was sent as Ambassador to Bologna. In 1379, he voted for the capital sentence of his own brother Giannozzo, implicated in the ill-fated Ciompi conspiracy. Franco Sacchetti is the author of *Trecento Novelle*, a collection of three hundred tales second only, for elegance and vigor, to Boccaccio's *Decameron*. He also wrote *Libro delle Rime* (Collection of Poems) and a humorous book, also in verse, entitled *La Battaglia delle Belle Donne di Firenze colle Vecchie* (Beautiful women of Florence at war with the old ones). Though lacking in scope and variety, his poetry is marked by an unmistakable charm. His woodlands and shepherdesses are always so fresh and alive that they seem to recreate, in a new and more personal atmosphere, the world of Theocritus, Moschus, and Bion. For even when they run the risk of monotony, his descriptions suddenly and gracefully take on an element of surprise in a last line or couplet, thus giving the poem an unforgettable incantation. The ballad which begins, "O lovely shepherdesses of the lea," is among the best-loved poems of the Italian language.

THE THORN-BUSH IN LOVE

A loving thorn-bush I had never seen
until the other day when I saw one.
On the green grass and under thorns and leaves
a sweet young damsel sat,
more shining than a star.
Whene'er the thorn-bush caught her golden hair,
she'd push it far away
with her white hand so fair;
but soon the thorn-bush would bend back once more,
bolder than all the bushes blooming there.
I'd never seen a fight of love before
such as that battle where
tresses were loosed and pretty features pricked.
Oh, at that moment many a hidden cry
many a time out of my heart came forth.
While I outside pretended but to laugh,
one wish alone I knew:
"Would that I could become a thorn-bush, too."

THROUGH THE WOODS ONE DAY

Pensively walking through the woods one day,
lasses I saw who gathered blossoms there,
saying, "Pluck that one there, pluck that one too,
right there, right there."
"What is it, what is it?"
"It's fleur-de-lis."
"For violets go there."
"Oh, I've been pricked by the thicket."
"Do not forget that one."
"Look, look, what is that, that is leaping?"
"A cricket."
"Come over here, come quick:
pick many a tuberose."
"But they're not those."
"They are."
"You,
you over there,
come here for mushrooms, here:
and there for thyme, right there."
"Let's not stay long, for the weather is changing:
it's lightning,
it's thundering,
the evening bells are ringing."
"But it's not even three."
"Listen, listen:
the nightingale is singing."
"I heard a better one,
I heard a better one."
"I think I'm hearing something."
"Where?"
"But where?"
"In that bush over there."

They search and they hit it and hit it,
and while the hitting grows,
a snake comes out of it.
"O me, poor me!"
"Poor me!"
And as they all are running full of fear,
the thunderstorm is here.
One—look—now slips, and one
falls, and one pricks her foot on a thorn:
garlands about are strewn:
one drops the blossoms picked, one treads on them,
and they're more blest who now can faster run.

That day, I, so enraptured, watched all that,
I did not realize I got all wet.

PASTORAL BALLAD

"O lovely shepherdesses of the lea,
whence do you come, so fair and full of glee?

"What is the country where you two were born,
that such sweet fruit so wondrously can bear?
Daughters of Love you look, such is the morn
that shines upon your brows and makes them fair.
No silver and no gold on you I see,
yet angels, poorly clad, you seem to me."

"Near a small forest on this Alp we stay;
a poor and tiny hut is all we own:
there every night we gladly find our way,
for Mom and Dad are waiting all alone.
Here for our sheep we care, as you can see,
and Nature cares for us, most tenderly."

"Greatly your beauty grieves, I dare believe,
that cannot shine outside this hilly place,
for of no regal home can I conceive
where you would not deserve man's highest praise.
Oh, tell me if you are content to be
so very poor on this your mountain lea."

"Both of us here are happier to go
behind our herds that pasture up and down
than any of you citizens would know
when going to your parties in your town.
No riches and no better destiny
but only buds and dance and song want we."

O Ballad, were I now a different man,
I'd be a shepherd on some mountain lea;
and before telling this to anyone,
where those fair lasses lived I'd love to be;
and now "O Blondie!," now "Martine!" I'd say,
following ever where they chose to stray.

41

EPIGRAMS

I

From hill to hill, from wood to wilder wood,
as a quick falcon, having long withstood
his master's ruthless hand, takes to the sky,

though still deprived of freedom, so go I,
wishing, O ladies, faster to depart
from him who grants you lordship on each heart.

Ah, but the farther I believe to be,
the closer I am still, and the less free.

II

The snow, the ice, and every morning gust,
coldness of hoarfrost, winds from alpine lair,
away Diana from her woods have thrust.

Seeing all grasses and all blossoms dead,
every leaf flying, every forest bare,
she wrapped a veil around her golden head,

and went back quickly to her native place,
leaving us burning for her blissful face.

Giovanni Dominici (1357-1419)

Born in Florence, Blessed Giovanni Dominici entered a Dominican novitiate at the age of seventeen. A learned theologian, he lectured in Florence and Venice during the last decade of the fourteenth century. He was made Archbishop of Ragusa, Sicily, and died a Cardinal, in Hungary. His extraordinary piety was officially recognized by the Church after his death.

Among his works, typical of the age in which he lived, is *Lucula Noctis,* a book of lucid though one-sided condemnation of Humanism as a source of evil especially among young men and women. His *Letters,* on the other hand, reveal the mystical aspect of his temperament.

The poem, "The Blessed Virgin and the Infant Jesus," attributed to him, is one of the most charming religious pages in Italian literature.

THE BLESSED VIRGIN AND THE
INFANT JESUS

Say, O sweet Mary, with how much desire
you gazed upon your son, my Christ, my Sire.

When without labor you to him gave birth,
I am quite certain the first thing you did
was to adore him, full of grace and mirth;
then on the hay you laid him in the crib,
and wrapped him round in humble raiments few,
and wonderment and joy, I know, you knew.

Oh, what great bliss, what ecstasy was yours
when you could hold him in your arms so tight!
O Mary, tell me (out of mercy you
should not perhaps deny me such a grace):
and did you then not kiss him on the face?
I know you did, and called him, "O my babe!"

You called him Son, and Father, and my Lord,
you called him Jesus, and you called him God.
Oh, what warm love within your heart you felt
when on your lap you suckled him at breast!
Oh, what caresses and what tender love
whene'er you were with him—your baby blest!

I do believe you suffered very much
when Jesus in the morn you had to dress,
for but in touching him your bliss was such,
you would not let him go from you away;
how you could bear all this, I fail to guess,
and how your heart did not desert you then.

If in the day he fell asleep awhile,
and you desired to waken paradise,
softly you went to him, who could not hear,
and bent your face upon his holy face,
and whispered then with your maternal smile:
"Oh, too much sleep can hurt you; sleep no more!"

Often, when he with other children was,
in haste, I think, you called your Jesus home,
to yourself saying, "You enjoy your playing,
but it takes something from my happiness."
And you would kiss him with so great a bliss,
no one felt ever such a love as you.

I have said nothing, nothing great or new,
in mentioning the least of all your joys;
but now a thought seems from my heart to rise
about your first and most sublime delight
 (I do not know how in so great a bliss
your heart did not burst open and soon cease) :

Oh, when you heard yourself called *Mamma*, how
did you not die of sweetness at that name?
How could you then withstand love's burning flame,
and soon not perish in its happiness?
Great your endurance must have truly been
if your existence did not finish then.

Our high Eternal Father called her, Daughter,
and with unending tenderness our Lord
called on this earth his humble handmaid Mother!
This thought alone makes my heart melt away.
Who wants to feel some sweet and tender spark
of this high love to which I ever aspire,
must place in my good Jesus all desire.

Anonymous (XV Century)

As every other nation, Italy has a great many literary gem
of which time has preserved only the luster. These two *ottave*
which could be by Guistiniani, are so charming in their fresh
naïveté, and so memorable in their delightful roguishness, tha
they seem a breath of pure air in an overcrowded room.

The original text of this poem comprises three stanzas. The
first of them, which seems to me the beginning of an altogether
different lyric, has been omitted.

PAPAL BLESSING

When you were born, O flower of paradise,
they brought you, to baptize you, right to Rome,
and when the pope uncovered your sweet face,
he your godfather wanted to become;
and then your mother, full of grace and fair,
gave you the name Diana like the star.

The Pope gave forty years' indulgence then
to everyone who simply looks at you;
hundred and sixty years of pardoned sin
to those who touch your dress; a person who
can talk to you, and kiss, my dear, your face,
goes, soul and body, straight to paradise.

Luigi Pulci (1432-1484)

The famous author of *Morgante* spent several years in the Laurentian circle. Lorenzo dearly loved his company and deeply appreciated the facility of his verse. Luigi, in turn, was so devoted to his master that, in one of his letters to him, he was able to say, "If you were here, I would make as many clusters of sonnets as there are cherries in this month of May." But even in the Medici household Luigi had his worries. Matteo Franco (1432-1494), Lorenzo's official chaplain, did not spare him in his caustic, vitriolic sonnets. Luigi tried to make his answers as vitriolic and caustic, but did not always succeed. The following lines, typical of Franco's aggressive and impudent muse, will give the reader some idea of the pettiness that surrounded the humanistic splendor of Lorenzo's Florence:

> If you, Luigi, I did dare insult
> by calling you a dog and parasite,
> you for an entire day, an entire night,
> have tried to fix your soup with your own salt.
> You on your brow your hunger so exalt,
> it seems a Giotto painting, pure and bright;
> and, wretched you!, you are in such a plight
> that not to care for you seems now my fault.
> But, though you with your hand and with a sheet
> rub more than once your pale and yellow cheeks,
> out of his tomb dead Lazarus I meet.
> Here at the Court, but bones your lordship seeks,
> or your last evening bells you soon will greet,
> whom Rubicant has craved for some long weeks.
> With Death you have played tricks
> eight days, and he has grown impatient so
> with his fast sickle, he forgives no foe.
> Limping, you, too, will go
> where Luca, the true thief you know so well,
> down in Judecca bids his brother dwell.

Luigi Pulci wrote, besides his *Morgante,* the *Beca da Dico mano* (an imitation of Lorenzo's *Nencia da Barberino*), a *Book of Sonnets, The Joust* (in which he celebrates the tournament won by Lorenzo in 1469), a *Confession* (a collection of poems in which he tries to defend his orthodoxy against charges of heresy) and *Letters.*

FROM *BECA DA DICOMANO*

I

Everyone sings of Nencia the night long,
and no one speaks of Beca in the least.
Because his Nencia's sung in hymn and song,
her dear Vallera ever calls her best.
But Beca is the fairest of the throng:
oh, look how well proportioned to the rest
her legs appear, and what a bud she is
that makes everyone's spirit melt in bliss.

II

My Beca's somewhat small, rather than not,
and limps a bit, oh, just a bit, I say.
She has in both her eyes a tiny spot
that, if you notice it, you soon call gay.
Around her little mouth there's some hair, but
it looks like a fresh trout out of the bay.
She's white like an old coin but—wait and see—
she only lacks a perfect husband—me.

III

Like wasps that, humming, humming the day long,
go round the grapes half ripe in the new light;
like donkeys wooing asses with their song,
all dandies come around you with a fight.
But, one after another, the whole throng
you hang like sausages—it serves them right.
O my dear love, if you could so pretend,
even the king you'd see before you bend.

IV

You're whiter than clear laundry or white lace,
more colorful than color, oh, much more
and more delightful than a market-place,
more prosperous than our great emperor,
more enterprising than our pastor's face,
more sugary than love and all that's for:
when in the midst of people you have fun,
still you are sober more than everyone.

V

Beca, are you aware of all my love?
The day I saw you in your bluish gown
depart for Florence, flourishing above,
 (and Ghilla wore your basket as a crown),
I felt a pricking all my spirit move
as if a drill were piercing up and down.
I said, "Like all the others you will, too,
dream of pomegranates more and more in view."

VI

Be patient, girls, as many as you are:
my Beca is the fairest of you all.
Her reason is a harpsichord by far,
and her blue skirt is more than I can call.
Oh, when she dances, what a graceful star!
Oh, what sweet grapes—and never mind the ball!
She moves her legs, and what am I to do?
I wish I could go higher than her shoe . . .

A SONNET

With him I, too, had supped one of those nights,
and got—what else?—a tench boiled more than once,
and other things that would have caused to dance
a rascal in the midst of his delights.
His waiters fell, and falls were their old rights,
although they blamed the staircase's expanse;
and all his wine was nothing but response
from barrel's bottom which no man excites.

The bread was merely flour of hazel-nut,
and some bad fat was offered us as pork
which was more eloquent than any thought.
Oh, the best peasant would have used a fork;
instead, I saw two hairy armfuls brought
that looked like the two talons of a stork.

       My host—oh, what a cork!—
tasted each thing in a delicious whirl,
and judged each course a most uncommon pearl.
       Ever with *z*'s and *erl*'s
he recommended all his birds, but I,
ignoring all his whispers, nearly died.

Il Pistoia (1440-1502)

Antonio Cammelli, known as Il Pistoia from the Tuscan ci
where he was born, spent some years at the Court of Ferra:
a town too genuinely enamored of epic lore to appreciate t
vein of his humorous verse. His poetry detaches itself fro
Burchiello's nonsensical brilliance, and paves the way for Bern
genuine, phantasmagoric realism. In an age when poets such
Cariteo, Tebaldeo, and Serafino Aquilano made havoc of I
trarchan themes, he reminded his readers of a tradition th
went back to Cecco Angiolieri, Cenne della Chitarra, and F
gore da San Gimignano. The three sonnets, here reproduce
may not represent him at his best, but are indicative of his fac
and often irreverent inspiration. He was not so ugly as
depicted himself; but his "Self-portrait" is in sharp contrast wi
the later self-aggrandizing sonnets of Alfieri and Foscolo.

SELF-PORTRAIT

Nature a hundred years had me in mind
to make a man as ugly as could be:
a thousand molds she made, unmade for me
until she could in Fear a model find.
My eyes and mouth she randomly designed
like one who starts a drawing drowsily.
This face of mine resembles none you see,
neither triangular nor square nor round.

My nose's tip is resting on my chin,
my whole complexion has the dark of night,
and—look!—my breast's where shoulders should have been.
From the waist down, two inches is my height:
one foot takes August, one September in,
and just as winding vine I stand up straight.
    When this great sculpture—wait!—
is finished, to the stick that I'll become
not owls alone—all birds will fly right home.

Note: This is a "sonetto caudato" (tailed sonnet). The "tail" is a peculiarity
the humorous sonnet. A short line rhyming with the fourteenth introduces a
plet of pentameters differently rhymed, and so forth. Often the "tail" is
ny times as long as the sonnet itself. "Tailed" sonnets were practiced by
ci, Pistoia, Berni, and even Michelangelo.

MATCHMAKING

"My daughter I would like to marry off:
for a good husband, Peter, look around."
"Madam, the perfect husband I have found:
no in-laws, she alone, with all that stuff."
"Rich?" "In his home his money's more than enough:
two vast estates, and what a site, what ground!
He dresses well, is virtuous and kind,
and never said a word you might call rough."

"He'll have a sweet young virgin in exchange,
who knows her mind, and who, in all her ways,
is honest, stable, fair, and never strange."
"But tell me now: What dowry can you raise?"
"A thousand ducats from the stock exchange,
and half of them in cash, here at this place.

So quicken, then, your pace,
and let the young man know and no more tarry:
let's sign the contract so the two can marry."
The schemer, in a hurry,
for his percentage brings the two together,
and for more money binds them with a tether.

ON CONTEMPORARY POETS

"Which Tuscan poets, say, seem good to you?"
"Tuscan or Latin?" "Both, it's understood."
"Lorenzo and his Piero are quite good,
but Poliziano's better than the two."
"Then?" "Benivieni's lyric labor's true;
extemporaneous Baccio Ugolino should
be mentioned." "Other Florentines?" "Include
Lapacin, Franco, Bellicioni, too."

"Who is in all of Lombardy the best?"
"Cosmico Paduan is a good source."
"No other?" "Count Boiardo 'mong the rest."
"Whom would you rate the third?" "My lord, of course."
"Fourth?" "Tebaldeo; but now let me rest,
for, of the moderns, these are the most terse."

           "Others from other shores?"
"There's Sannazaro, who calls Naples home;
Sasso in Modena, Serafin in Rome.
           I would explode a bomb
if I began to numerate them all:
each day the entire calendar should fall."

Matteo Maria Boiardo (1441-1494)

Born at Scandiano (Reggio Emilia) of noble descent, Boiar
spent most of his life with the Este family of Ferrara. Politi
intrigues and private animosities were the causes of an attem
on his life in 1474. He married Taddea Gonzaga di Novella
in 1479, and the following year was made Governor of Modena
Ercole d'Este. He was also Governor of Reggio, where he di
The last stanza of his unfinished masterpiece, *Orlando Innam
rato,* is full of tragic sadness:

> While I am singing, O Redeemer God,
> I see all Italy become one blaze
> under these French who come most valiantly
> to raze and pillage I know not what place.
> Therefore I leave you with this futile love
> of Fiordispina burning deep and low;
> some other time, if God more sunshine sends,
> I'll tell you quickly how the story ends.

His minor works, both in Latin and Italian, were deeply inf
enced by Petrarch; but some of his sonnets and ballads have
felicity of phrase and a depth of feeling uncommon to the poet
of the fifteenth century. The line, "Yet the eternal anguish
can bear," breaks loose from all literary imitation and describ
a deeply felt inner truth.

EIGHT SONNETS

I

I saw the sun rise from the sea, one morn,
clothed with a frightful mane of golden rays,
and such live sheen did all his face adorn
that every shore around him seemed ablaze.
I saw a rose, soon after, being born
to the first dew, so flaming in its gaze
that one who watched it from a distant place
thought of a fire upon some verdant thorn.

In the same season that buds first on earth
I saw the fresh frail grass reburgeon bright,
just as it shot its very first leaves forth.
But then a fair and winsome lass I met,
gathering roses in the primal light
and with her beauty vanquishing all that.

II

Young shepherdess—behold—leads to the plain
the white-wooled flocks that in her keeping are,
seeing the sun go down (for it is late)
and smoke arise from chimneys very far.
Until now bent, the ploughman—look—stands straight
and gazes on the quickly fleeting day,
then hurriedly releases from their yoke
his oxen, and now moves to rest away.

But I, alone and shelterless, although
the sun now pauses, with my thoughts am still,
and come once more to sigh with every star.
O dear distress of love, how sweet you are:
sunshine or darkness, never can I rest,
yet the eternal anguish I can bear.

III

Who from a bird takes song and wings away,
and from a blossom color and perfume,
and from the grass the honor of its bloom,
and from a meadow buds and bushes gay,
and from a deer its antlers' branching height,
and sun and stars and splendor from the sky,
he can forbid a gentle heart to sigh,
and rob new love of all its hope and light.

For without love man's heart is without hope—
a tree devoid of boughs and of new leaves,
a river with no water down its slope.
Love takes all sadness from the soul away,
and all the bliss that in man's nature heaves
goes to a heart in love, therein to stay.

IV

O charming little window, where is she
who with her luster used to make you bright?
Your loss seems not to grieve you, I can see,
but, oh, how much you should lament with me!
You're nothing now without her gentle glow,
for bids are withered, violets are dead;
no longer has the day its sun to show
nor has the night, without her, stars to shed.

Yet I remember that you were, one day,
mid marble white and many a colored bloom,
adorned with her—herself a blossom gay.
Love used on yonder balcony to be,
who now has left you in your lonesome doom,
to keep his home in her fair company.

V

"Discolored flowers and pallid violets,
swayed by the wind with motion soft and fair,
where did your Mistress go? Oh where, oh where
did the Sun go, who used to give you light?"
"Our Mistress with the sun has fled away,
who used to show us beauty ever new;
and since elsewhere so great enchantment flew,
bare our distress and misery we lay."

"O hapless flowers and grieving violets,
now so deserted by that warmth divine
which made your sight so colorful and gay!"
"How true! Within our roots we feel the loss,
and you within your heart now feel the harm,
which brings to the same end both you and us."

VI

Give me, full-handed, roses, give me lilies,
scatter around me violets and buds;
let each who once with me bemoaned my sorrow
now come and share the fruit of my delight.
And give me flowers, vermilion and white:
only bright hues for such a day are best.
And fragrances of love around me cast,
so that this place and my desire be one.

Forgiveness,—my sweet foe now grants me peace,
and wants me to be living from now on,
she who alone of wondrous mercy boasts.
So wonder not that I by fire am won;
marvel at this alone—that still my heart
is not in all such happiness undone.

VII

The sky shines not more sweetly to our eyes,
when fair with splendors that the night brings down,
nor the enchanted trembling of the sea
lustrous and tranquil in the rising sun;
nor that star dripping from the space above
with dewy freshness in the morning prime,
nor a sun's beam that, scattered, sparkles back
on gleaming ice or whiteness of hoar-frost;

nor does in heaven anything more gentle
and lovable burn bright, or breathe on earth,
that to itself alone allures our gaze,
as does the graceful and enamored sight
of those fair eyes which Love makes move and turn:
who doubts all this, he dares not face their light.

VIII

The singing of the birds from leaf to leaf,
the fragrance of the breeze from flower to flower,
and now the glitter of a dewy shower
to make our sight more blissful and more blest—
it is because both Nature and Heaven love
this lass, who bids the world love her in turn:
that's why sweet song and scent fill skies above,
that's why both earth and sea themselves adorn.

Wherever she may walk, or turn her glance,
such is the warmth of love she kindles there,
we feel before its time its radiance.
At her sweet smile, at her sweet gazing bright
the grass blooms green, each flower is painted fair,
the sky turns limpid and the sea grows quiet.

MADRIGALS

I

As in the clear liquidity of night
the star of Love before daybreak appears,
so full of splendor and of golden rays
as to adorn the horizon with its light;
and out it comes, ahead
of other lesser stars
which soon around it spread
and yield part of the sky, and bow to it;
then, from its dewy tresses raining down
a liquid luster bathing
the green new grass and every colored bloom,
it makes the countryside one thing of dew:
so does this lady, going out with Love,
outshine all other women's merit bright
and blot all other beauty from man's sight.

II

Sing, O you lovely birds in love, with me,
since it is Love now bids me sing with you;
and you, clear rills that sinuously flow
through banks in bloom anew,
with this my poem your soft answer blend.

So boundless is the beauty that I sing,
my heart does not dare bend
to such a task, alone,
for it is weak and weary for such weight.

Wandering little birds, you now take flight
perhaps because you think
my heart is laden with lamenting fright,
and fail to guess my feeling of distress.

Wandering birds, then heed:
however round the sea,
however strong the winds that blow and hiss,
there is on earth no bliss
that can be equal to this joy in me.

Lorenzo De' Medici (1449-1492)

"In a wonderful manner he loved all those who excelled in some art, though his preference was for men of letters. This can be strongly confirmed by Agnolo da Montepulciano (Poliziano), Cristofano Landini, and Greek Demetrius. For this reason Count Giovanni della Mirandola, a being more divine than human, prompted by Lorenzo's munificence to abandon all the other lands of Europe through which he had been wandering, finally chose Florence as his dwelling place. In an admirable way he delighted in architecture, music, and poetry, and many poetical works not only composed but also expounded by him are still extant. And so that the young people of Florence might engage themselves in the literary disciplines, he opened in the city of Pisa a University to which he attracted the most notable scholars of Italy. It is hard to think of any vices that might have stained so many virtues in him, though he was deeply involved in erotic matters, and took delight in facetious, mordant groups, and childish games, far more than it seemed worthy of so great a man, who many a time was seen participating in the amusement of his own sons and daughters. Indeed, one who observed his life, voluptuous as well as austere, noticed two different personalities blended through a nearly impossible conjunction. He lived the last years of his existence in the utmost discomfort because of an ailment of the stomach that through unbearable pains brought him to death in April, 1492, in the forty-fourth year of his life."

Thus Machiavelli describes the Magnificent in the last chapter of his *History of Florence*.

Lorenzo wrote *Canti Carnascialeschi, Canzoniere, Selve d'-Amore, Ambra, Corinto, I Beoni* (a parody of Dante's *Comedy* and Petrarch's *Trionfi*), *Caccia col Falcone, Canzoni a Ballo, Rime Spirituali, San Giovanni e Paolo* and, probably, *Nencia da Barberino*. Always brilliant and musical, his verse often disguises the deep and complex restlessness of his spirit.

LEAVE YOUR SO MUCH BELOVED
ISLAND HOME

Leave your so much beloved island home,
leave your fair kingdom of so much delight,
O Cyprian goddess; and upon the stream,
bathing the greenness of this young grass, come.
Come to this shade and to the pleasant breeze
that makes a song of every tender tree,
and to the loving lay of every bird;
and now let this, your chosen country be.

And if you come among these limpid rills,
take your beloved, darling son along,
for in this place his worth is unknown still.
Take from Diana all her modest nymphs,
who, free from peril, loose, about are faring,
little for Love and all his virtue caring.

LET THOSE WHO CARE, HAVE POMP
AND HONORS HIGH

Let those who care, have pomp and honors high,
temples and squares and palaces aloft,
and treasures and delights, all followed by
a thousand woes, a thousand vexing thoughts.
A little meadow green, full of fair blooms,
a rivulet that wets the grass around,
an amorous little bird in tearful sound—
all this far better all my passion calms;

and shady woods and rocks and mountains high,
and deep dark caves, and animals astray,
and some fair nymph appearing, sweet and shy.
There with my quick and wandering thoughts I see
those beauteous lights as though they were alive;
here, this or that takes them away from me.

TO SLEEP

Sleep, O most balmy sleep, come down at last
into this anguished heart that longs for you;
close the unending spring of tears and rue,
O bland oblivion never coming fast.
O come to me, my only peaceful rest,
which can alone check my desire, and here
bring as your mate my lady sweet and dear
with those calm limpid eyes where mercy's best.

Show me the happy smile the Graces chose
as their new home, and let one pitying glance,
one wary word, stir my desire no more.
If thus you show her to me, let our sleep
eternal be, or let these joyful dreams,
ah, never venture through the ivory door.

ON VANITY

How vain is every hope upon this earth,
how false and empty are our human plans,
and how the world is full of ignorance—
Death, supreme teacher, shows to everyone.
Some live in song and tournament and dance,
others to a fair face with all thoughts run;
some scorn both world and worldly circumstance,
others show not without what's deep within.

Vain cares and thoughts, so different a fate
as Nature grants in her variety,
one sees each moment in this world astray.
Everything flees and a short while can stay,
so mobile is among us Fortune's wheel:
but Death within eternity stands still.

SESTINA IV

I shun the fair rays of my ardent Sun,
like a wild beast within the shade of leaves,
and go in quest of rivulets and fountains
through shores and valleys and through lofty hills,
wherever the chaste nymphs of fair Diana
chase all the beasts away throughout the woods.

Beneath the shading beeches in the woods
I try in vain to shun the burning sun,
for even in the kingdom of Diana
I fail to hide among the verdant leaves
from the harsh fire that fears no shade of hills
and is not tamed by limpid waves of fountains.

But now my tears replenish all the fountains
which, bathing and restoring the green woods,
leave silver traces on the highest hills;
yet never does the fire of my bright sun
abate, while greener all the amorous leaves
rebloom in the fair kingdom of Diana.

I thought that by the magic of Diana
I would forget my smart, and living fountains
would quench my flames, and that the shade of leaves,
which I go seeking through so many woods,
would shield me from the rays of the clear sun,
and this would be less strong in vales and hills.

But fire is every breeze on yonder hills;
my thoughts obey the magic of Diana,
and the farther it is, the worse the sun;
and 'tis but fire the water of cool fountains,
nothing but fire the shade of all dark woods,
and fire are waves and shades and trees and leaves.

For, ah, although I lay among the leaves
this mortal weight of mine, and on the hills,
and though I chase wild animals through woods
and fields in the fair kingdom of Diana,
and seek a shelter under trees and fountains,
my heart can never be far from the sun.

As long as the sun fill with light the leaves,
and fountains leave their traces on high hills,
throughout the woods I will pursue Diana.

SONG FOR DANCE

O fair lasses, long around
have I looked for my heart lost.
But, O Love, I thank you most,
for my heart I now have found.

In this dance perhaps is she
who did steal it from my breast:
hers it is and will it be,
while in me my life shall last:
she's so kind and heaven-blest
that she'll ever hold it bound.
But, O Love, I thank you most,
for my heart I now have found.

O fair lasses, shall I say
how my heart I now have found?
When I knew it ran astray,
I began to look around;
soon two lovely eyes I met,
where my heart was safe and sound.
But, O Love, I thank you most,
for my heart I now have found.

Now what pain must this thief face,
who did steal my heart like this?
Oh, how fair and full of grace!
How she brings love in her eyes!
Her I never will release:
let her heart burn, with mine bound.
But, O Love, I thank you most,
for my heart I now have found.

Bind, O Love, this thief indeed,
burn her with the thing she stole:
if she begs you, do not heed,
do not look at her at all;
let your darts and arrows fall
till my heart revenge has found.
But, O Love, I thank you most,
for my heart I now have found.

TRIUMPH OF BACCHUS AND ARIADNE

Oh, how lovely youth can be,
that is fleeing fast away:
if you care to be, be gay:
what's to come we cannot see.

Bacchus and Ariadne fair
deep in love are with each other;
time deceives and flies like air:
they're forever gay together.
All these nymphs, all people rather,
ever merry want to stay.
if you care to be, be gay:
what's to come we cannot see.

All these Satyrs, glad and shrewd,
much in love with these nymphs fair,
in each cave and in each wood
now have laid their hundredth snare:
spurred by Bacchus, everywhere
dancing, leaping—look—are they.
If you care to be, be gay:
what's to come we cannot see.

All these nymphs (I tell the truth)
love to fall into those traps:
people thankless and uncouth
against Love can guard perhaps.
Intermingling sounds and steps,
now they sing and now they play.
If you care to be, be gay:
what's to come we cannot see.

Look, this weight that comes behind
is Silenus on an ass.
Old and fat and almost blind,
he is drunk and glad: alas,
he can hardly stand and pass,
yet with fun he laughs allway.
If you care to be, be gay:
what's to come we cannot see.

Midas comes behind these all:
what he touches soon is gold.
What its wealth, and what its goal,
if it leaves you sad and cold?
What contentment can man hold
if his thirst will ever stay?
If you care to be, be gay:
what's to come we cannot see.

Let all people heed me then:
on the morrow no one feed,
but let women and let men,
young and old, know today's need:
to be glad and chase, indeed,
every sadness fast away.
If you care to be, be gay:
what's to come we cannot see.

Loving lads and lasses, come:
long live Bacchus, long live Love!
Dance and sing and beat your drum!
Let your hearts all sweetness prove!
Never toil and never grieve!
Fate will always have its way.
If you care to be, be gay:
what's to come we cannot see.

SONG OF GIRLS AND OF CICADAS

The Girls

We are women, as you see,
youthful lasses fair and gay,
and are seeking our delight
for this is Carnival day.
Envious people and Cicadas
much resent an alien glee;
so they vent their evil rancor,
the Cicadas that you see.
Most unfortunate are we!
The Cicadas' prey we are:
the whole summer chattering,
they still chatter the whole year:
and from those who do far worse
comes the worst of gossiping.

The Cicadas

O fair lasses, we but do
what within our nature is;
often, though, the fault is yours,
for it's you who tell all this.
One must act, but also know
how to hide one's happiness.
One who's quick can run away
from the peril of the word:
does it pay to make one die
in a long, long agony?
Without chattering too much,
act at once, while you still may.

The Girls

What's the purpose of our beauty?
It's worth nothing if it goes.
Long live love and gentleness!
Death to envy and Cicadas!
Want to gossip? Very well:
we shall act, and you will tell.

FROM *LA NENCIA DA BARBERINO**
(9-11, 13, 17, 20)

My Nencia is perfection out and in:
she's white and rosy, tall as she should be,
and has a dimple, yea, right in her chin,
which makes her figure quite a thing to see.
And she has feelings just as she has brain.
So charming and remarkable is she,
she's the best thing created in heaven above
with which a million men should fall in love.

Yes, sir, a lucky man, indeed, is he
who such a pretty thing one day will marry;
born under a lucky star, who such a fleur-de-lis—
all blossom with no leaves—will pluck and carry;
blesséd and holy that one man will be,
who will recover from desire and worry—
holding at last that face, not any other,
white, soft, and tender like a lump of butter.

Oh, Nencia, if the great great love you knew,
which for the luster of your eyes I bear,
and also the great pain and smarting woe
as if my teeth were all at once pulled out;
if this you knew, your heart would break, no doubt,
and you would let all other suitors go,
and love but your Vallera, me alone,
for you're the one my heart desires to own.

* Some modern critics attribute this rustic poem to Bernardo Giambullari.

When in a group of men I see you go,
the only thing I do is to be close;
and when I see that someone looks at you
it seems that out of me my whole heart goes.
Across my heart so deep and deep you sit,
it makes me every moment sick with sighs,
and sick with sobs and tears, so sad and great,
which, as they flow, I send out to you straight.

Nenciozza dear, I should this Saturday
travel as far as Florence, there to sell
two loads of wood I chopped but yesterday
while calves and cows were grazing calm and well.
Think of the thing you want me there to buy,
if something I must get you, big or small—
perhaps some lipstick or perhaps some powder,
hairpins or a few cents of needles, rather.

O bud of mine, I now must say goodbye,
for—look—my cows are near my home already:
I have been chatting much too much, and hope
I have left none still grazing on the meadow.
They have just crossed the river, I can see,
and I hear Mona Masa calling me.
Be well and happy: singing, I depart,
forever calling Nencia with my heart.

TO JESUS DEAD

O malicious, hardened heart,
source of every wicked thought,
you should break within my breast,
and by grief be torn apart.

Be by nothing comforted,
O my heart as hard as stone,
for sweet Jesus now is dead.
World is trembling, sun is spent;
from their graves the dead come out,
and the Temple's veil is rent.
Heaven and earth are weeping, but
you feel nothing, hardened heart!

Melt, oh, melt like wax away,
O my wicked, impious heart,
for the One True Life is dead,
your own Jesus, loving Lord.
O my heart, on His hard cross
be with Jesus crucified,
and may that same spear pierce you,
which has piercéd Jesus' side.

O my heart, when wounded thus,
may your tears a torrent be,
like the blood that from that Holy
Side is gushing copiously.
O my heart, he feels great bliss,
who with Holy Jesus is!
If so sweet the pain you feel,
death with Him is sweeter still.

Such sweet water's pouring forth
from such source of bitterness!
Since, O God, you so loved death,
death is now sweet happiness.
O my heart, from Jesus learn:
take and carry your own cross,
and on it be crucified:
he dies not, who with Him died!

Girolamo Savonarola (1452-1498)

The man who even today appears to some critics and historians as the dark, avenging shadow of the Middle Ages was the very one who saved the Medicean library for Florence and the world. He was not against the humanistic light; he only wanted Saint Augustine, Saint Jerome, and the Holy Writ to be read along with Vergil, Homer, and Cicero. In his *First Decennial* Machiavelli referred to the fiery Dominican from Ferrara as

> *... the great Savonarola*
> *Who, spurred by divine breath of inspiration,*
> *Kept you all bound to his prophetic word.*

Whether a fanatic or a prophet, an ambitious demagogue or a saintly moralist in a century of political and ecclesiastical corruption, the monk who from the Florentine monastery of Saint Mark thundered against Lorenzo de' Medici and Pope Alexander VI belongs to the history of Florence and of the Church. Excommunicated, hanged, and burned at the stake, he continued to live in the minds of those who had heard his sermons. Every religious parenthesis in the erotic poetry of the Renaissance re-echoes a line or a thought of Savonarola's "Songs of Penance."

EXHORTATION TO HIS SOUL

Adown a wicked pathway
my soul is seen to be,
and, if no help is coming,
she will die presently.

It is the devil cheats her
with his mendacity,
it is the senses promise
a bliss that cannot be,

and still the world allures her
to more iniquity:
my soul, so tried and tempted,
who will once more set free?

Help, wretched thing, thyself with
the gift God granted thee:
thou hast free will to live by
and make thy merit be.

Oh, run to Christ thy Jesus:
nailed on a cross is he;
he'll save thee if thou beg him
with great humility.

Have faith and hope, and strengthened
by him thou shalt soon be.
Without thy will, no power
can ever conquer thee.

Grace is a stronger weapon
than all adversity.
Think but of death, how quickly
it will descend on thee;

and think of hell, how fully
torturesome it will be,
and then look up to heaven
and all its ecstasy.

By fervor new be kindled,
replete with charity,
and every pain and burden
will seem quite light to thee.

Thy sweetest bridegroom Jesus
will wed thee finally,
and with his gentle kisses
will kiss thee tenderly.

Thy mind, of life eternal
shall taste a guarantee:
thy heart shall hear the festive
songs that are yet to be,

"Love, O my Love," then singing,
"Love, highest piety!"
So, tread upon the pathway
God has revealed to thee,
praising God One and Only
in Holy Trinity.

O SOUL, BY SIN MADE BLIND

O soul, by sin made blind—and sorely robbed of rest,
God hates in you mankind—for this your life unblest;
your bridegroom, Jesus Christ—you've lost indeed,
nor do you plead—for pity, help, or peace.
> Alas, alas, alas,
> fear of the Lord is dead in us.

In Prato and in Bibbona—a thousand signs are shown,
yet not the smallest corner—new faith can light and own;
on vice your mind alone—is still intent:
what punishment—will soon against you pass!
> Alas, alas, alas . . .

Italy is at war—and famine finds new room;
the plague wins every shore—and spreads God's wrathful doom:
such is the food of gloom—left for your blind,
lost life, mankind—of faith as frail as glass.
> Alas, alas, alas . . .

Prophets, astrologers—learned and saintly men,
preachers with sermons terse—your woes had in their ken;
yet madly over again—you sing and play
your sinful way: —virtue's no more with us.
> Alas, alas, alas . . .

Tell me each gift and grace—God did to you assign;
how many thoughts, not base—did in your heart once shine,
and how much help divine!—But, thankless still
you are of will—and sloth too deep to pass.
> Alas, alas, alas . . .

Go back to Jesus Christ—and to His Mother dear;
no more by vice enticed—desert your path of fear.
Our Virgin Mary's near—and full of grace:
tears on her face—she begs her Son for us.
> Alas, alas, alas,
> fear of the Lord is dead in us.

Leonardo Da Vinci (1452-1519)

Leonardo, the most versatile genius of the Renaissance, called himself "omo sanza lettere" (man without letters) either to detach himself from Petrarchism or to protect against verbiage the sacredness of his scientific beliefs and visions. He never wrote poetry that we know of. Yet with this page, "In Praise of Water," he started what we often refer to as "poetry in prose." Reconstructed by several critics according to its rhythm and natural cadences, this passage, though neither hymn nor ode, is, as Francesco Flora observes, a felicitous proof of the manner in which scientific analysis and poetic description achieved in Leonardo a unity of beauty and awe.

IN PRAISE OF WATER

Water is Nature's vehicle.

She can never pause until she be one again with her own element, the sea, where, molested by winds no more, she settles down and rests with her surface equidistant from the center of the world.

She is the augmentation and lymph of all living bodies. No sublunar thing can hold its primeval form without her.

She binds and increases all bodies, and makes them ever grow.

No lighter thing can without violence penetrate her.

She willingly rises through heat in thinness of vapor.

Cold air freezes her, stability corrupts her.

She takes on every smell, color and taste, and has nothing fully her own.

In her swift course she becomes the upholder of things much heavier than herself.

With motion and leap she can rise to the sky.

When down she comes, she submerges into her own ruination things much lighter than herself.

Water is weightless on her bottom unless she strike it.

Water unmakes mountains, fills valleys, and would like to make of the earth a perfect sphere—if she could.

She wears out the loftiest mountain peaks.

She uproots and removes great rocks.

She chases the sea from its ancient confines, for with the debris she brings she raises its bottom.

She breaks and ravages height of shores.

No firmness can ever be seen in her that does not suddenly change its nature.

With her rivers she yearns for declivities of valleys, and here she takes away and there she adds new soil.

Therefore many rivers are said to be those through which the whole element has passed,

and many times have they given the sea back to the sea,

and no part of the earth is ever so tall as not to have had the sea at its bottom before,

and no profundity of the sea is ever so low as not to have be
    the base of tallest mountains before.
She is now sour and now strong,
now brusque and now bitter,
now sweet and now thick or thin;
and she looks now harmful or pestiferous,
now salutary or venomous.
Therefore she has as many natures, so we say, as is the varie
    of the places through which she passes.
And as a mirror becomes the color of its object, so she becom
    the nature of the place through which she goes:
salutary,
harmful,
soluble,
stagnant,
sulphurous,
salty,
sanguine,
sad,
shuddering,
wrathful,
red, yellow, green, black, blue,
oily, fat, lean.
Now she causes fire, now she extinguishes it—warm, cold;
now she takes away, now she gives,
now she digs and now she raises,
now she wrecks and now she builds,
now she empties now she fills,
now she soars and now she plunges,
now she runs and now she rests,
now she causes life or death, conception or annulment,
now she feeds and now she starves,
now she's salty, now insipid,
and now with her great deluges she sinks the ample valleys.

ıw she bends toward northern parts, corroding the bottom of
   their dams,
w toward noon she destroys the opposite shore,
ıw she turns toward the center of the earth, consuming the
   bottom that balances it,
w with burgeoning ebullitions she leaps against the sky,
w with circular rotation she alters her course,
ıw from the western parts she looms, taking the harvest away
   from the farmers,
ıw from the east she discharges the theft of the soil.
ıd so, she digs and fills, she steals and gives back.
ıd so, now turbid and rabid she flows with her fury; then lucid
   and tranquil she plays with fresh young grasses, pleasantly
   going.
ow from the sky she falls with rain or snow or hail, now with
   thin mists she forms thick clouds.
ow by her own, now by alien force she is moved,
ıw she augments things born with lymph of life,
ıw she shows herself fetid or fragrant.
'ithout her nothing can ever be found among us.
ow she is part of the warm element and, as vapor, is one with
   the air and, pulled by the heat, goes up, and there, reaching
   the cold region, because of her opposite nature shrinks
   together with the minute particles clinging to her.
ıd as the hand that dips a sponge underwater until, having
   absorbed all the water possible and being all flooded with
   it, the sponge gives all of it back through its fissures,
. the cold squeezes the warm humidity which, having been
   turned into a denser form, causes the air enclosed in it to
   break the weaker part with violence,
ıd it blows as though it really came out of bellows pressed by
   excessive weight.
nd so through different sites she chases the lightest clouds she
   meets along her opposite paths.

· ·

Have you ever seen water come down from the cut branches
    the vine, fall on its roots and, penetrating them, rise on
    again?
Thus, falling into the sea, water penetrates the bowels of tl
    earth and, resuming the might of her motion, rises on
    more with violence and, following her natural inclinatio
    descends and returns.
So, recomposed and made one once again, with endless revol
    tion she turns now within now without,
and now by accident soars, now by nature descends.
So up and down, within and without,
she knows no solace ever, either in her direction or her substanc
and, like a mirror, she becomes the color of the objects throug
    which she has passed.
Nothing she owns, but all she moves or seizes,
and takes on so many natures as is the variety of the plac
    through which she goes.

Girolamo Benivieni (1453-1542)

Close in his youth to Lorenzo de Medici, with whom he ex-
anged conventional Petrarchan sonnets, Girolamo Benivieni
came the exponent of Marsilio Ficino's neo-platonic theories
a *Canzone dell'Amore Celeste e Divino,* which had the honor
a commentary in three books by Pico della Mirandola. The
me Canzone was known to Spenser, who freely echoed some
its stanzas (those reproduced here) in his *Fowre Hymnes.*
ıt, aside from the influence of that poetic tour de force, which
sures him of a place in the literary history of the Renaissance,
nivieni was a minor Petrarchist even when, under the spell
Savonarola whose doctrines he had come to espouse, he de-
led to rewrite some of his early compositions as religious verse.
is known that one of his *Laude* was sung at the Bonfire of
arieties during the Carnival of the year 1497.

87

From THE SONG OF CELESTIAL AND DIVINE LOVE

Love, from whose hands the bridle of my heart
is hanging, and in whose most holy reign
he did not least disdain
to start the flame that was to fire it all,
Love moves my lips, and forces this my brain
to speak of him, and what my burning smart
conceals; but this my heart
fails, and my tongue heeds not so rare a call.
Yet I must try my concept to express:
no human strength can win a greater might.
But since Love promised his own pinions bright
to my dull mind when into this my heart
he first came to alight,
no more to leave from there but there to rest
and build his newer nest,
if his live splendor my true escort be,
I hope now to make known what hides in me.

I'll tell how Love out of the source divine
of uncreated Bliss comes to man's earth;
wherefore and when he has birth,
moves heavens, molds our souls, and rules the world;
how from the human heart he spreads his worth,
bearing sharp weapons as his battling sign,
and how he makes us pine,
and bids this human flock go heavenward;
how his flames burn and scald, and with what law
he turns them high, and the enflamed one bends,
or keeps both hanging still between the two.
My weary rhymes, O sad, ill verses, you,
see that his might on earth I make full bare,
so that the worthier prayer
of this my kindled heart may Phoebus win.
Too harsh my yoke has been:
the promised feathers to my weary wing
give, Love, or on his way this blind man bring! ...

As soon as the first Good's eternal mind
lives, comprehends, and, comprehending, moves
man's soul, it paints and gives
that very sun that fires the divine breast:
so all a pious heart holds and conceives
flows from above, and feelings, so assigned,
wondrously then man's mind
lives, comprehends, and moves to its effect.
From it, in turn, as from God's intellect,
Venus down here is born, whose beauty glows
in heaven, lives on earth, and dims the world.
The one, that's in the Sun, mirrors itself
but in the shade of Light that, blinding, grows;
so all its riches flows
from the live luster that within shines bright.
Thus to man's soul all light
comes, and, as heavenly love decreases in it,
it bends on vulgar sheen that very minute.

As soon as, shaped to come upon this earth,
the soul departs from God's own face, it starts
down from the highest parts
where the sun dwells, till in man's heart it hides.
There, it reveals with the most wondrous art
the light brought down from its own star, that worth
which, parcel of its birth,
still feeds on all its prime inheritance,
and in the human seed can so advance
as nature strives, for there it builds its home
in ways that often Heaven do not win.
Therefore, from the same sun, that's carved within,
God's molten imprint to man's heart does come:
now if the soul become
one with that flame, the light that dwells in it
by divine rays is lit,
and made more fair by virtue from above:
thus a sweet error feeds a heart in love. . . .

A SONNET

When Love saw all the luster of those eyes
extinguished, whence his worth was wont to start,
several times, in vain, he aimed his dart,
eager to see my wounds and hear my cries.
In vain he bent his bow, weak and unwise,
in vain his impious arm flew at my heart,
for safe I lived, and healed of my old smart,
or still too sated with my ancient sighs.

Disdainful, then, he took (how wrong are those
who think they'll ever shun his fatal wrath!)
a better bow, and the right time he chose
to wound me: from live rock a laurel tree
uprooting, in my heart he forced it: there,
mid verdant boughs, he sits, and laughs at me.

Angelo Poliziano (1454-1494)

One of the most accomplished humanists in the Laurentian circle, Angelo Ambrogini, better known as Poliziano, was born in Montepulciano. At the age of ten, after the tragic death of his father, he went to Florence where among his teachers he met such scholars as Marsilio Ficino and Argyropulos. At nineteen, he was invited by Lorenzo de' Medici to tutor his children at his Palace, which he had to leave, six years later, having displeased Clarice Orsini, Lorenzo's wife. The following year, however, he was readmitted to the Palace, and was given the chair of Latin and Greek at the University of Florence. In 1493 Pope Alexander VI rejected Lorenzo's proposal to give Poliziano the Cardinal's hat.

In honor of Giuliano de' Medici and Simonetta Cattaneo he wrote the *Stanze per la Giostra,* which he left unfinished when the Pazzi conspiracy claimed Giuliano's life. In Mantua, while a guest of the Gonzagas, he composed in two days the fable *Orfeo,* which was performed with great success. And in Latin he wrote, among other things, Odes, Epistles, Epigrams, and Elegies.

Inferior to Lorenzo's for sincerity of initial inspiration, Poliziano's verse surpasses it in grace of diction and elegance of color. His phrase always has the limpidness of that classical light which was, indeed, Poliziano's second nature. He is the poet of the rose, which he describes in the transience of its fragrance.

From LE STANZE, Book I

XXV

Zephyr, adorned already with fair blossoms,
had banished from the mountains all the frost;
the weary pilgrim swallow, little swallow,
had flown already back into her nest;
with tenderness the murmur of the woods
ever around the morning hour was heard,
and the laborious bee, at the first sheen,
preying on this and on that bloom was seen.

XXVI

Undaunted Julus at the daylight's prime
when owls resume their clayey solitude,
on his new-bridled, proudly running steed
started with chosen friends out toward the woods
 (and under good command came right behind
the close-knit pack of many a faithful hound),
all bearing that which with the hunting goes—
arrows and horns and spits and traps and bows.

XXXVII

He was already, as he had desired,
from his companions far and far away,
and saw his steed already out of breath
just as he was one step behind his prey;
but still pursuing all his hope in vain,
into a verdant blooming mead he came.
There a gay nymph whose veil was waving white
appeared to him and soon was out of sight.

XXXVIII

Out of his sight the forest phantom fled,
and for the nymph the youth seemed not to care;
rather, he checked the bridles of his steed
and stopped him right upon that greenness fair.
But, full of wonder, he was seeing still
the fleeting figure of the nymphet there,
and a new sweetness then seemed to depart
from her fair eyes and fall into his heart.

XLIII

Full white is she, and white her dress is too,
though painted all with roses, grass, and flowers:
the golden ringlets of her golden hair
stream down upon her brow that's humbly proud.
The forest all around him is one smile
and does its best to quiet his despair.
Majestic in her bearing and yet meek,
she with one glance can tame all tempests quick.

XLIV

A limpid sweetness in her eyes is flashing,
where Cupid keeps all of his torches hid;
the air about her shines with joyous glow
whene'er she turn her glances' loving light.
With heavenly happiness her face is lit,
with privets and with roses painted bright:
all breezes listen to her heavenly words,
and sing a Latin of their own, all birds.

XLVII

Upon that greenness she was gladly sitting,
and she had woven a small gentle wreath;
her dress was painted with as many blossoms
as all about her were by Nature made.
But as her glances rested on the youth,
somewhat bewildered, lifted she her dress
and, holding up its hem with her white hand,
with blossoms on her lap was seen to stand.

LV

Then with more smiling and more joyous eyes,
whereby she made the sky above grow bright,
slowly she moved upon the youthful grass,
each step an act adorned with loving grace.
Soon a sweet keening from the forest came,
and the small birds began to weep and weep;
but under her lithe tread the grass became
white, blue, and yellow, and vermilion flame.

WELCOME MAY

Oh, welcome May
and its flag wild and gay!

Welcome, oh, welcome Spring
that bids men love anew.
And you, your lovers bring,
all of them, maidens who
with buds and roses new
adorn yourselves in May,

and come to the cool bliss
of bushes green again.
Safe each fair maiden is
among all these young men;
for birds and beasts all burn
with love when here comes May.

No fair and youthful lass
should cruel be today,
for youth, unlike the grass,
cannot find back its way:
let none of you be harsh
to her sweetheart in May.

Now let each sing and dance
of these our merry bands.
Sweet lovers—look—advance
to the joust for your hands;
if harsh to them, one rends
the blossom that is May.

To win a damsel's heart
each loving youth wears shield.
To those who love and smart,
beautiful maidens, yield!
Give back the hearts concealed,
and wage no war in May!

Who stole a heart, let her
give her own in exchange.
But who is flying up there?
'Tis Love, the wondrous angel,
who comes, fair maidens, down
to praise with you the May.

With rose and lily crowned,
and for your lips athirst,
Love, laughing, comes aground.
Welcome him to your feast.
Who will, of you, be first
to give him buds of May?

Oh, let the pilgrim stay.
Love, what's your bidding now?
Each damsel fair must lay
a wreath on her lover's brow;
and women all, though old,
must fall in love in May.

BALLAD OF THE ROSES

Sweet lasses, one fine morning in mid-May
I happened in a garden green to stray.

Lilies and violets were all about
on the green grass, with other blossoms new,
yellow and blue, vermilion and white.
I quick stretched out my hand to pick a few
so as to wreathe my blond hair with their hue,
and crown my sweetheart's brow with garland gay.
Sweet lasses, one fine morning of mid-May . . .

But as I plucked more flowers than I could handle,
roses I saw of many colors fair:
I ran to gather them and fill my mantle,
for their sweet fragrance was so fresh and rare
my heart awoke in gladness then and there,
borne by desire and heavenly bliss away.
Sweet lasses, one fine morning of mid-May . . .

I wondered then; oh, never could I tell
how beautiful those roses were indeed:
some were still burgeoning with a sweet smell;
others were new; and others somewhat dead.
Love said to me, "Go, gather those which need
upon their native thorn no more to stay."
Sweet lasses, one fine morning of mid-May . . .

When the rose opens all its petals, when
it is most lovely, when it is most dear,
then it is good for garland or for chain,
before its beauty starts to disappear.
So, lasses, while its bloom is high and here,
come to the garden, pluck your rose today.
Sweet lasses, one fine morning of mid-May . . .

PASTORAL LAY

Listen, at least ye woods, to my sweet lay,
for, ah, my nymph is deaf to all I say.

My lovely nymph is deaf to my lament
and for my sounding pipe she does not care:
my hornèd flock, to show its sad complaint,
shuns the pure water of the rill down there,
and does not want to touch this grass so rare,
so much it feels its shepherd's great dismay.
Listen, at least ye woods, to my sweet lay.

The flock is of its shepherd very fond,
but this nymph seems to scorn her lover's moan;
this beauteous nymph has heart of adamant,
harder, that is, than iron, harder than stone:
away she ever runs from me alone,
as a lamb, frightened, from the wolf away.
Listen, at least ye woods, to my sweet lay.

Tell her, my pipe, how nimble beauty goes
away forever with our falling years;
and tell her, time destroys all human joys,
and youth, when lost, never again appears;
tell her, she should use well her beauty dear,
for violets and roses do not stay.
Listen, at least ye woods, to my sweet lay.

Bear, O ye winds, this melancholy sound
right to the ears of the nymph I adore;
and tell her how my days with tears abound,
and beg her to be cruel, ah, no more:
tell her, my life flies fast away, as hoar-
frost flees and dies beneath the sun's warm ray.

Listen, at least ye woods, to my sweet lay,
for, ah, my nymph is deaf to all I say.

BACCHANAL

Bacchus, let all follow you!
Bacchus, Bacchus, *live anew!*

If you care to drink, come, fellows,
come to drink and come right here.
Make big barrels of your bellies,
and I'll join you—have no fear.
For you, too, there's wine, my dear.
Who comes first to drink? I do.
Bacchus, let all follow you.

I've already gulped my horn:
fetch the flask that is in stock.
Look, these hills begin to turn,
and my brain now takes a walk.
Here and there let all these folk
spin and run, just as I do.
Bacchus, let all follow you.

I am dying for some sleep.
Am I drunk, say yes or no?
Straight my legs no more can keep.
It is you are drunk, I know.
Everyone do as I do:
everyone do as I do.
Bacchus, let all follow you.

Everyone shout Bacchus Bacchus,
and still swallow more wine down,
till our noise be weak and raucous.
Drink! You too, you too, drink down!
I can't dance another bout.
Live anew let all men shout.

Bacchus, let all follow you!
Bacchus, Bacchus, *live anew!*

I THANK YOU, LOVE

I thank you, Love,
for all distress and pain,
and now am glad I have in sorrow lain.

I now am glad for all I have endured
in your fair realm, O lord,
for not through my desert but through your grace
have I been granted such a lofty pledge,
and thus made worthy of
a smile of such delight
as to uplift my heart to heaven above.
I thank you, Love.

To heaven above my heart has been upraised
by those fair smiling eyes
wherein, O Love, I saw you full-concealed
in all your glowing flames.
O gleaming gentle eyes
that stole my heart away,
whence do you such rare faculties receive?
I thank you, Love.

I was already on the brink of death;
my lady, clad in white,
came soon to save me with a loving smile—
humble and glad and fair,
roses and violets
a crown around her hair,
her eyes out-dazzling the bright sun above.
I thank you, Love.

EVERYTHING OR NOTHING

Let all sing, and I will too:
what a song from me and you!

I of promises am weary:
tap your barrel now I must.
You have kept me feary feary,
giving crickets for a crust.
After all this "deary deary,"
this my fleeting eel can flee.
"Firefly, firefly," then you'll query,
"come right back!"—but deaf I'll be.

So I'll try to pierce and puncture
that your wine I'll drink today.
When I'm finally all rapture,
'tis Saint Anthony of May.
You are leading me your way
like a blockhead by the nose;
pipe or drum no longer goes—
oh, no more, my dear, I say.

We have done so much of cooing
there are those who call us crazy.
If our game's not our undoing,
you'll see something quite amazin'.
As you know, no terror stays in
Love's sweet dwelling much at ease:
halfway in and halfway out—
you call bliss and I call doubt.

RISPETTI*

I

This lass of mine, so gay and so quick-fiery,
turns all of me into an ashen diary.
The things she says or does, make my mouth watery,
and all her deeds and winks become my treasury.
Consumed by flames, my heart's a whining article:
would that I had of all her grace a particle.
like spawning fish I've frolicked in my ditch,
and now you keep me, Love, deep in your pitch.

II

Oh, of your beauty, lady, do not boast,
for but a whiff can blot it out of sight.
The golden hair that seems to crown or fill
your lovely features will turn gray and white.
So, pluck your bud while it is luscious still,
for beauty can a fleeting moment last.
Fresh is the rose at dawn, but when night comes
suddenly all its loveliness succumbs.

III

When you will see my eyes forever spent
and to its other life my spirit flown,
oh, how I hope you'll bitterly lament
the cruel fate of my existence gone:
for only then, aware of your great blunder,
will you feel sorry for me, buried under;
but your remorse in vain will make you sigh:
therefore, my lady, do not make me die.

* A "rispetto" is a short love poem, usually of eight or even six lines, which originated in Tuscany. Most of its charm is in its light tone and colloquial nature.

IV

When in a flash your glorious face appeared,
and your sweet voice for the first time was heard,
turned into paradise, the whole earth cheered,
and where you passed, the sun its flags unfurled.
If now, alas, I gaze into your glances,
no longer is your face what this mind fancies.
Where did your dear and dazzling beauty fade?
Oh, what a costly lesson, I'm afraid!

Iacopo Sannazaro (1455?-1530)

Born in Naples, and called the Neapolitan Vergil, Sannazaro is the author of two important literary works, *Arcadia* and *De Partu Virginis,* in Italian and Latin, respectively. The former, a mixture of prose and verse in the fashion of Dante's *Vita Nuova,* is a pastoral novel, the real focus of which is not the unhappy youth meditating on unrequited love, but rather the idyllic atmosphere of Arcady. Sannazaro opened, indeed, for Italian literature the new horizons of pastoral poetry. A man of placid nature, he served King Frederick with silent devotion, and in his villa at Mergellina—a gift from his king—found the tranquillity he needed for the creation of his impeccable Latin eclogues, elegies, and epigrams. When the Prince of Orange destroyed his "nest," the poet shared with his King the bitterness of exile from Naples. When he returned to his native city in 1504, he sold his property in order to publish his *Arcadia.* He died in Naples, and was buried in the Church of S. Maria del Parto and S. Nazario, which he had built near his villa.

The province of Sannazaro's *Arcadia* with all its green meadows and grazing sheep, its shady trees and murmurous hills, its pipes and shepherds' whispers, was to become in the two following centuries a languorous world of literature.

ON THE DEATH OF ANDROGÈO

Beautiful, blessèd soul,
that, free from earthly weight,
flew bare above to your supernal home,
where now, once more made whole
with your own star, you're bright,
and can rejoice, and scoff at this our doom,
shining, a sun in bloom,
among the brightest souls;
now with your holy glow
'mid wandering stars you go,
and 'mid fresh fountainheads and sacred myrtles
you tend your heavenly herd,
guiding from high your shepherds with your word.

New mountains and new plains,
new rills and youthful trees,
and newer blossoms in the sky you see:
old Sylvans and old Fauns
to places new within the summer ease
follow their nymphs for a more loving glee.
Thus, in the scent he'll be
tenderly heard as he still sings between
Daphnis and Meliboeus—
our Andr020020202020 Androgèo dear.
Listen! he fills the sky with sweetness new,
softening right and wrong
with the clear sound of his compelling song.

As to the elm the vine,
and to the herd a bull,
and to a happy field the golden wheat,
such did your glory shine
when this our throng was full.
Ah, cruel Death, who'll save us from deceit,
if with your flames you set
the tallest peaks ablaze?

Who in the world will name
a shepherd of such fame
that, singing here among us such sweet rhymes,
may once again restore
the woods with leaves and shades that were before?

The holy Nymphs all kept
on mourning your youth gone:
rivers and dens and beeches know it well.
The banks, once verdant, wept,
and the pale, withered grass; for days, the sun
the tragic news could tell,
and the wild beasts of the dell
refused all grass or lawn,
and flocks were no more seen on hill or mountain,
so much they cried for your untimely fate;
and, during day and dusk,
Androgèo Androgèo each wood would ask.

Therefore, fresh wreaths upon
your sacred sepulchre,
and shepherds' vows you will forever see;
and so, each season gone,
like a new dove astir,
from shepherds' lips to lips your name will flee;
and never will it be
that your fair fame may fade on earth or die,
till serpents be concealed
deep in their lairs or in their rills the fish.
Now you alone in this my weary word
will live, as in this song
the sound of countless rhymes, and shepherds' throng.

If any sense of love among you lives,
O oaks so green and dense,
oh, gently shade these soft-interred remains!

ICARUS

Icarus perished here: these very waves
know it, which on their lap took those wings splendid;
here the race finished, here the great deed ended,
which will be envied by all future men.
Oh, anguish most unique and lucky, then,
if, dying, he attained eternal fame!
And blessèd he, who such a death could claim,
so fair a prize rewarding loss and pain!

Happy in his abyss he now should dwell,
who, scanning like a dove the firmament,
lost, for his daring, light and breath as well.
For now so wide a sea—this element—
re-echoes his audacious flight, astir:
who had on earth so vast a sepulchre?

Serafino Aquilano (1466-1500)

Serafino de' Ciminelli, born in Aquila of the Abruzzi region and therefore known as the Aquilano, was the brightest star in the literary horizon of the last decade of the fifteenth century. His fame almost eclipsed Petrarch's. To hear him recite his own poems to the accompaniment of a lute, which he played skillfully was a memorable experience. There are several accounts of his performances in Rome, Urbino, Mantua, Milan, Naples, and other cities. Foreign poets such as Wyatt and Surrey knew his poetry and translated it. He was an angel to some, a charlatan to others; but, undoubtedly, he possessed a magnetism which Petrarch himself would probably have envied. Of Petrarch he knew, though superficially, every secret, and what he knew he succeeded in making his own. His death (he was only thirty-four years of age) was mourned in hundreds of poems in Greek, Latin, Italian, and Spanish. The following utterly baroque sonnet by Annibale Poggio from Bologna is taken from a commemorative anthology published by Giovanni Filoteo Achillini in 1504:

> As Serafin performed in Rome, one day,
> so sweet and wondrous was the song he sang
> it shook the entire city from its base,
> and all its crumbling parts around him came.
> 'Twas then the Fates, alas, cut off his thread,
> for such was the commotion and uproar
> of palaces and domes his song tore down
> that he was smothered by them instantly.
>
> Thus lifeless Aquilan beneath their ruins
> is buried, he who in one fleeting hour
> brought on himself and Rome such dismal death.
> Therefore, O reader, all the broken walls
> you see around you tell you they were felled
> by Serafin, whose end the whole world mourns.

Even the dissenting Bernardo Dovizi da Bibbiena had to admit, in the last line of his sonnet on Serafino's death, that "one man alone possessed the gifts of many."

108

TO A BLIND BEGGAR

Blind man, who come here begging for some bread,
humbly lamenting with a cry of woe,
you're not the only one to suffer so,
for human fate in many a form we dread.
Once I was whole and healthy; now, instead,
with neither eyes nor heart around I go,
guided forever by a sightless foe,
whereas by your still faithful dog you're led.

You're asking for some food, I for my heart;
much pity for your wrong you ever gain,
but none can give me what I beg in vain.
You have your heart and soul; I'm dead in part:
be therefore happy, thinking of my case,
for a worse harm can smaller ones erase.

THE TRIPLE WEALTH

Let each surrounded citadel call *me*,
if all its water supplies are cut or fail;
and you, man, born ever to cross the sea,
call me, f still you need wind for your sail;
let those who with no fire in winter be
shivering, call for me, and joy'll prevail:
three things a-plenty gave me Love, my sire—
to my mouth wind, to my eyes water, to my heart fire.

109

A RIDDLE

I am the one well-known to but a few,
and this my foot the whole blind world puts under.
I fix and waste and lower, raise, renew
what the Sun watches in its daily wonder.
Without my aid you, men, can nothing do;
Nature and Fortune but to me surrender.
So swift on all creation are my wings
that what you grasp is nothing but dead things.*

* The answer is: Time

Niccolò Machiavelli (1469-1527)

The author of *The Prince* not only wrote verse but resented not having been mentioned by Ariosto among the many poets praised in Canto 46 of *Orlando Furioso*. When he fell in disgrace with the Medici, he pleaded for his freedom not in the name of justice but of poetry. Yet in a moment of self-criticism he called himself "one who gathers buds at the foot of Helicon." Although he knows all the flowers blooming at the base of the sacred mountain, he seldom weaves a perfect garland. Most of his verse lacks that undefinable yet unmistakable essence of great poetry. His ratiocinative power often overwhelms his feeling and makes him see, not recreate, the world around him. His passions and dreams remain his own and fail to represent universal dreams and passions. This is because Machiavelli, though a dreamer by nature, does not allow himself to be carried away by his dream. He always explains but seldom suggests, so that paradoxically his verse loses strength as it gains in clarity. Despite all this, Machiavelli's poetical production should not be dismissed, for it is in his verse that one can see a Machiavelli without his Roman toga and unaware of being watched among his noisy friends at the Inn of San Casciano.

He was the first of the great Italians to be buried in the Church of Santa Croce in Florence.*

---

* See my book, *Lust and Liberty: The Poems of Machiavelli*, from which the following poems have been taken.

TO GIULIANO, SON OF LORENZO DE' MEDICI

I

I wear, Giuliano, chains instead of shoes,
and round my shoulders goes a rope six times,
and I won't tell you all my other woes
since thus are treated those who deal with rhymes.
Along these walls I see such squat lice climb,
they look like butterflies, so fat they grow.
Neither at Roncesvalles nor in the slime
of the Sardinian woods was ever so

sordid a stench as in this dainty place;
and so the noise is harsh, I do believe
Aetna and Jove are thundering in the space.
One is being chained; another, soon to leave,
is being freed with bang of bolts and keys;
high from the floor, another wants reprieve.
But this made me most grieve:
I was aroused (the dawn was peeping through)
by voices singing, "We do pray for you."
In peace, oh, let them go:
but you, good father, oh, do not refuse
your mercy, and break soon this evil noose.

II

Last night, as I was begging all the Muses
to deign to visit, with the soothing strain
of their sweet harp, Your Lordship, and again
present to You my most humble excuses,
one of them, sneering, said to me: "Whose voice is
this daring cry?" My name I told her, then;
and she, to make more desolate my pain,
shut my mouth, left on my face many bruises,

and said: "You're Dazzo, indeed, not Niccolò,
with all those ropes around your legs and toes,
for only some big fool can be chained so."
I wished to tell the reason for my woes,
but this is what she answered: "You can go
to hell—you and your play, foul and verbose."
Oh, may You testify,
Magnificent Giuliàn, for God on high,
how Dazzo I am not, but I am I.

III

I'm sending you, Giuliano, if I might,
several thrushes—a small gift, I guess,
but good to make Your Lordship think a bit
of your poor Machiavello in distress.
And if around you, you have men who bite,
I beg you, force into their throats all this,
so that, while eating of these birds, who knows!
they may stop rending someone's name and right.

But you will say, "How can these birds achieve
all that, being not good or fat at all?
My men of touching them would not conceive."
Then let me tell you this: as they recall,
I too am thin, yet of my flesh they leave
no inch untried by their teeth's hungry fall.
Oh, answer not the call
of empty words, my Lord; and judge and see,
not with your eyes but with your hands, my plea.

CHANCE*

"Who are you? Surely not a mortal thing,
with all this grace God has bestowed on you.
Why restless so, and on each foot a wing?"

"I'm Chance, and but to few myself reveal.
Mobile forever, I forever go
because I spin upon a spinning wheel.

"No one can fly as fast as I can run;
and I have wings around my feet, so that
my never-ending speed all men may stun.

I show before me my disheveled hair,
wherewith I cover both my face and breast,
so that you may not know when I am there.

"The back of my head utterly is shorn:
therefore, in vain you try to grab me when
I pass you by or, just around you, turn."

"Tell me: Who's coming in your company?"
"Her name is Penance. So remember this:
he conquers her, who fails to conquer me.

"You fool, who cannot even see or guess
that, having asked these futile questions, you
have lost all of your time in idleness!

I am no more within your reach or view."

* This poem is an adaptation of Ausonius' Epigram XII, "In Simulacrum
:casionis Et Poenitentiae."

Pietro Bembo (1470-1547)

Born in Venice, Bembo was the greatest literary authority
the first half of the sixteenth century. His word was law, an
his sonnets were hailed as the most significant achievement sin
Petrarch. Petrarchism found in him its most brilliant and con
petent exponent, so much so that Petrarchism and Bembis
came to signify one thing. So impeccable a Latinist as to becon
Pope Leo X's secretary, he advocated the cause of the verna
ular tongue by suggesting that it should imitate the vigor, el
gance, and realism of its three fourteenth-century masters.

In his *Asolani*, dialogues written before 1505, he himself po
tificated on Platonic love. His classical erudition knew no bou
daries, and a few fortunate friends took advantage of it b
entrusting to him the literary education of their children. A
the dawn of the sixteenth century he fell in love with Lucret
Borgia. Made a Cardinal by Pope Paul III in 1539, he wa
Bishop of Gubbio in 1543, and of Bergamo in 1544. He died
Rome.

On Petrarchism in general and Bembo in particular, Fran
cesco Berni waged the relentless war of his parody in whic
he ridiculed golden tresses, ivory hands, divine speech, an
Cupid's darts. But Bembo's *Canzoniere*, which was indeed
model of highly polished versification, contained also momen
of poignant sincerity.

ON THE DEATH OF HIS BROTHER

And have you, too, now left me in your prime,
bereaved of you, my Brother, through your death,
causing my life which once knew light and mirth
to turn to darkness and to martyrdom?
It would have been great justice if your dart
had struck on me, for this I wanted most,
and if, as I was first to come down here,
I had been also first hence to depart.

For I would not have seen my own great loss—
the sudden flight of the best part of me—
and would now be with you far from this woe.
But since ahead of you I could not go,
may the Lord grant, Who does not love deceit,
that I, unburdened, soon may follow you.

ON THE DESCENT OF CHARLES VIII
OF FRANCE

Part of the world, so dear to God before,
closed by bleak rock and girded by the water,
O sweeter, happier land than any other,
marked and divided by proud Apennine:
to what avail have the good sons of Mars
left you as sovereign on both land and sea?
Throngs, once your slaves, wage war on you today,
and now their hands on your loose tresses lay.

Even among your children there is one
who, calling these most alien swords against you,
into your beauteous body thrusts his own.
Now, are such deeds the glories of our past?
Is this the way we honor land and God?
O hardened age! O seed all gone to waste!

WHEN THE SUN LEAVES US

When the sun leaves us, maybe to make room
for all the stars, and when our sky grows dark,
flooded with them which, fair and lustrous, bloom,
first one, then ten, and soon a hundred sparks;
I think and ask myself in which of them
that very moment glows the one whom none
could match beneath the circle of the moon,
though much of Laura the world speaks and knows.

And her I mourn; and when I go to rest
again, a larger river floods my eyes,
and soon her image inundates my soul
which, sadly looking and with fixèd glance,
tells her the things that I dare not relate:
O bitter nights! Unjust and impious Fate!

A CURLY HAIR OF GOLD

A curly hair of gold and amber pure and bright,
flying within the breeze and waving on the snow;
two eyes of gentle grace, much brighter than sunglow,
which turn to limpid day the blackness of the night;
laughter that calms all grief and heavy bitterness;
and pearls and rubies whence so tender words come forth
that nevermore the soul desires an alien bliss;
ivory hands that steal men's hearts and hold them tight;

a song which truly seems a harmony from heaven;
maturity of wisdom in the greenest years;
gracefulness ne'er before revealed to human view;
the highest virtue with the highest beauty bound:
all this lit up my fire, and these are then in you
"the graces which few ladies by lavish God are given."

118

MADRIGAL

When on the smarts I muse,
which you, O Love, still give me, harsh and strong,
toward death I run, and long
in such a way to finish all my woes.

But as I stand before
the limit of this sea of bitterness,
such is my happiness,
my soul grows brave, and I cross not, therefore.

Thus, living gives me death,
and death restores me once again to life:
O my unending grief,
which one brings on, the other takes not off!

Ludovico Ariosto (1474-1533)

The author of *Orlando Furioso*, the greatest Italian poem aft
the *Divine Comedy*, was born in Reggio Emilia. In 1501, o
year after his father's death, he was nominated Captain
Canossa. In 1503 Cardinal Ippolito d'Este, Bishop of Ferra
appointed him his secretary. The failures of his diplomatic m
sions to Pope Julius II, in 1509 and 1512, marked the end
his dream of an ecclesiastic career in Rome. His refusal to acco
pany Cardinal Ippolito to Hungary is vividly narrated in t
first of the three Satires included in this Anthology. In 1522
was nominated Governor of the Garfagnana, a region heavi
infested with bandits, and there he performed his administrati
duties with admirable success. When he returned to Ferrara
married, in great secrecy, Alessandra Benucci. In 1532 he m
Emperor Charles V in Mantua and presented him with a co
of *Orlando Furioso*, then in its third edition. Carved above t
door of the little house, which he had bought in Ferrara, w
the Horatian motto, "Parva sed apta mihi." His *Satires* sh
us Ariosto as he really was or wanted to be—a proud, indepen
ent man in love with literature and a quiet life. Provincial
taste but highly sophisticated and fastidious in his quest of l
erary excellence, Ariosto raised the Italian language to its ul
mate peak of fluency and melodiousness. Realistic, biting, cool
ironic, free of rhetorical excesses, his *Satires* are nourished l
his experiences.

Ariosto also wrote comedies, the best of which does not atta
the level of Machiavelli's *Mandragola*, probably the greatest pl
of the Italian Renaissance.

From SATIRE II

I wish to be informed by both of you,
dear brother Alexander, Bagno dear,
if I am still remembered at the Court;

if by our lord I still am blamed; if friends
arise in my defense and tell the truth—
why, when the others went, I chose to stay;

or if, experienced in flattery,
 (the art we study and we worship most),
you help him blame me more than I deserve.

He is a fool who contradicts his lord,
even if he should say he saw the day
flooded with stars, and at midnight the sun.

Whether he praise or whether he despise,
several voices make one melody
at once, from all the men he has around;

and he who out of modesty dares not
open his mouth, applauds with all his face,
and seems to say, "I, too, agree with you."

But if for other things you blame me still,
you should at least admire the fact that I,
who chose to stay, said so with frankness bold

and with no subterfuge. Several reasons,
all of them true, I had, each in itself
mighty enough to keep me where I am—

life, first of all, which still I do prefer
to other things, and do not wish to make
shorter than heaven or my fortune wills.

The slightest aggravation of this trouble
of mine would either kill me or soon prove
both Valentin and Pòstumo quite wrong.

Doctors have spoken, yes, but I myself
know more than any other my own ills,
and what is good and what is bad for me.

I know my nature does not well agree
with rigid winters: and beneath the Pole
they are far worse than here in Italy.

And not the cold alone would do me harm—
also the heat of stoves which I detest
much more than from the plague I'd run away.

Nor is harsh winter in that place of yours
spent far from them: you eat and play and drink,
and do up there everything else but sleep.

Who leaves those stoves, how can he breathe the air
which is forever kept in great unrest
by the cold winds from Ural Mountains near?
Vapor, which from my stomach comes and turns
to catarrh in the head, then seeks my chest,
would some night choke me—and goodbye to me.

And fuming wines, which I must shun far more
than poison, there you gulp at every visit,
and to drink little is great sacrilege.

And all your dinners, spiced with cinnamon
and pepper and much else, are not for me,
for they're most harmful, as my doctor says.

But you might tell me I could find up there
some corner near the fireplace where I could
keep feet and armpits dry, and would not burp;

also, your cook would have for me alone
such meals as I desired, and I might drink
a bit of watered wine or none at all.

In other words, you would be all together,
and I from dawn to evening all alone
down in my cell, and like a monk at table!

I would need pots and other crockery
for kitchen and for bedroom, and utensils
such as are brought as dowry by new brides.

If master chef Pasino will oblige
to make a special dish a couple of times,
four and six times his eyes will shoot at me.

. . . .

But I, alas, have reasons not to come.
The first you know; if I should tell them all,
this sheet and then the next would not suffice.

And yet another should be mentioned: I
must not allow our home to crumble down,
should all support be suddenly removed.

Of the five children, Charles is in that realm
whence my Cleander was by Turks cast out,
and where he plans a little more to stay.

Galasso wishes in Evander's town
to don a surplice on his cassock soon;
and for your lord you, Alexander, left us.

There's Gabriel here: but what do you expect
of one who has from childhood (ah, sad fate!)
remained without the use of arms and feet?

Never outdoors, never to court went he,
and you can understand what all this means
to one who wishes to support a house.

For our fifth sister who is still at home,
now that she is to wed, there is the need
of her own dowry, which we owe to her.

Our mother's age is, then, the thing that rends
my heart with grief, for she cannot at once,
without our shame, be left by all of us.

I am the first of ten, already old
at forty-four, and for some time I have
hidden my baldness underneath a wig.

So, for this bit of my remaining life
I do the best I can; but you, who came
out of that womb eighteen years after me,

go back to visit Germans and Hungarians,
follow your lord in winter and in summer,
serve for me, too, and, oh, restore my loss!

If he wants service of both pen and ink,
and lets me stay in this my tranquil den,
tell him, "My brother is your own, my lord."

While staying here, I will with bugles clear
make soon his name resound perhaps so high
as dove could never on its pinions soar.

As far as Filo, Cento, Ariano, and Calto,
I'll gladly go, but to the Danube no:
for such a jump my feet have not the strength.

Were I to weave again around the spindle
the fifteen years I spent in serving him,
I would not hesitate to cross the Don.

If having given me every four months
twenty-five crowns—and they were not so steady
as not to be contended many a time—

means that he has to chain me as a slave,
force me to sweat and tremble, with no thought
that I might die or anyway fall ill,

do not allow him to caress this hope;
tell him that, rather than to be his slave,
in patience I will bear my poverty.

There was a donkey once, so very lean,
he showed but nerve and bone; and he went through
a broken wall to where some wheat was heaped,

and ate so much of it, his belly grew
bigger than a big barrel, till he was
full sated, although not immediately.

But fearing, then, lest someone break his bones,
he tried to leave just as he had come in,
but now the hole seemed much too small for him.

While he was panting to get out in vain,
a little mouse thus told him, "To go out,
get rid, my friend, of that big belly first;

you now had better start to vomit all
you have in you, and thus be thin again,
or you will never make it through that hole."

So, in conclusion, let me say that if
our Sacred Eminence thinks that I am bought
with all his gifts, I'll gladly give them back

and thus resume the freedom that was mine.

From SATIRE III

One saddle or one burden cannot fit
all backs: to one it seems no weight at all,
another is oppressed and vexed and crushed.

A nightingale can hardly bear a cage,
a finch can longer last, and more a linnet,
but in one day a swallow dies of rage.

Let those who long for spurs or for a hat
serve king or duke, or cardinal or pope;
not I, who little care for this or that.

A turnip that I cook in my own home,
and put, when cooked, upon a stick, and peel
and sprinkle then with vinegar and must,

to me tastes better than wild boar and thrush
and partridge elsewhere; and beneath a cheap
blanket I lie as though it were of silk

and gold. Here I can rest my weary limbs
instead of boasting they have been in Scythia,
in India, Ethiopia, and beyond.

Men's appetites are varied: there is one
who likes the tonsure, one who likes the sword;
one likes the country, one the distant shores.

Let those who want to travel, go ahead:
let them see England, Hungary, France, and Spain;
I like to live right here in my own land.

I've seen Romagna, Lombardy, and Tuscany,
the mount which crosses, and the one which closes
Italy, and both seas by which she's bathed.

This is enough for me: the rest of the world
with Ptolemy I'll travel, without paying
for rented rooms, in time of peace or war;

and safely, on the maps, and without raising
my vows to God when thunders break the sky,
I'll sail the whole sea, better than by ships.

. . . .

Someone will say that, had I gone to Rome
to hunt for favors, I would have already
caught more than one into my very net,

considering I was among the old
friends of the Pope's, before his worth or luck
made him sublime upon the highest seat.

And long before the Florentines to him
opened their doors, the day his Giuliano
fled for a shelter to the Feltro Court,

where with the one who shaped the *Courtier*,
with Bembo and others, dear to god Apollo,
he made his exile a less grievous lot;

and even afterward, when in their land
the Medici got cocky, and the Gonfalon,
fleeing the Palace, knew its fiercest shake;

until he went to Rome to be a Leo,
so dear was I to him, he made me think
he loved few people more than he loved me;

and several times, as Nuncio and in Florence,
he told me, should the need arise, between
me and his brother he would see no difference.

That is why people think there is no doubt
that, if I were in Rome, I now would don
the hat that's green inside and black outside.

To those who so believe I shall reply
with this example. Read it: it is easier
for you to read it than for me to write it.

There came a summer once, when so the soil
was burnt, it seemed the Sun had once again
yielded his horses' reins to Phaëton.

Dry was each well, and every fountain dry,
and rills and ponds and the most famous streams
one could have crossed without a bridge's aid.

There was a shepherd in those very days,
rich (or should I say saddened?) with a number
of herds and flocks, among all shepherds poor.

After he searched for water in each cave,
ever in vain, to that high Lord he turned
who never cheats those who have faith in Him;

and inspiration lighted then his heart
that he would find the longed-for water down
the bottom of a valley, not too far.

With wife and sons and all he had on earth
right there he went, and with his servants there
he found the water without traveling much.

But as, to draw it out, he found himself
with nothing but a small and narrow bucket,
he said, "You will not mind if I drink first,

"and my wife second; and my children then
come third and fourth, as it should be, until
the thirst is quenched that scorches each of them.

"Then all my servants, but one at a time,
must forward come to drink, according to
the labor each has put to dig this well.

"Then we'll decide about each beast I own,
and let all those whose loss would hurt us most
have on the others precedence of care."

Obeying such a law, each went to drink,
and each, not to be last, began to boast
and magnify the merits that were his.

Seeing and hearing all these things, a wench,
who by the master had been dearly loved
and much enjoyed one day, screamed: "Woe to you!

"I'm not his relative, nor have I helped
digging the well; yet I can't give him more
than what I have already given him;

"and here I see myself the very last,
and I shall die of thirst if I don't try
to find for my salvation some new stream."

Dear cousin, with this anecdote get rid
of those who think the Pope would soon prefer
me to a Neri, a Vanni, a Lotti, a Bacci.

His nephews and his relatives—not few—
are first to drink; and then come those who helped
him don the fairest mantle of them all.

When these have drunk, it will be dear to him
that those should drink who helped him to return
to Florence and, for that, fought Soderini.

One says: "I stood in Casentìn with Piero,
and ran the risk of being caught and killed."
"I lent him money," soon Brandino shouts.

Another says: "His brother I supported
one entire year, and gave him clothes and arms,
and helped him with a horse and with my cash."

If, until all have drunk, I wait to quench
my thirst, I won't be thirsty any more
or I shall find the well without one drop.

Better to stay in this my tranquil place
than know the truth, that one whom Fortune lifts
to heaven, into Lethe first is plunged.

But, though mankind be there immersed, it's true
she kept this man alone far from that stream
which cancels every memory of the past.

I can bear witness to the things I write,
for, when for the first time I kissed his foot,
I did not find him short of memory.

Toward me he bent out of his blessèd seat,
and took my hand and then both of my cheeks
and placed on each of them his holy kiss.

He even kindly gave me half a bull,
the other half of which Bibiena dear
has expedited at my own expense.

Then with my heart and with my mantle full
of hope, but soaked with rain and soiled with mud,
I went to sup at the Montòn that night.

Let's say 'tis true the Pope remembers all
that he has promised, and now wants to give me
the fruit of what I've sown for many a year;

let's say 'tis true he'll give me just as many
mitres and diadems as in the chapel
Jonah sees people at the Papal Mass;

let's say 'tis true he'll fill with gold my pockets,
my sleeves, my lap and, if it's not enough,
my throat, my belly, and my vitals, too:

will, for all this, that boundless greed for wealth
be quenched in me? and will my thirsty snake
be satisfied with all these things at last?

From Morocco to China, from Nile to Dacia,
not just to Rome, I'll go, if I can be
granted the grace of sating my desires;

but, should I be a Cardinal or even
the Servant of all Servants, and see still
no limit ever for my stubborn greed,

what would the goal of all my sweating be
in climbing all those rungs? Oh, better much
to stay and rest and to perspire much less.

Upon that time when still the world was new,
and the first crowd was innocent and good,
and there was not the shrewdness of today,

down at the foot of a high mount whose peak
seemed to touch heaven, in a valley lived
a throng the name of which I do not know.

Several times they saw the climbing moon,
with horns and now without, now full, now waning,
go round the sky in its accustomed way;

and thinking that from the high mountain peak
they would succeed in seeing how it grew
and how it shrank into itself once more,

one with a basket, with a sack another,
up to the summit they began to run,
vying, and eager, all of them, to see.

But as they could not any closer come
to the far moon, they all fell weary down,
wishing in vain they had remained below.

And those who saw them high from the low plain,
believing they were touching now the moon,
were seen behind them with a hurried step.

This is the mountain of the wheel of Fortune,
upon whose top ignorant people think
that there is every peace—but there is none.

. . . .

From SATIRE VII

There was a pumpkin once, which soared so high
in a few days, it hid the tallest part
of a pear tree that happened to be nigh.

The pear tree, which had slept a long long sleep,
opened its eyes one morn and, seeing those
strange fruits upon its summit resting deep,

asked: "Who are you? Up here how did you climb?
When I, awhile ago, gave up to sleep
my weary eyes—where were you at that time?"

The pumpkin told its name, and showed the place
below where men had sown it: in three months
it had climbed there by quickening its pace.

"I," said the tree, "could hardly reach this height
by bearing in the heat and in the frost
against all winds full thirty years of fight.

"But you, who in a wink can reach the sky,
now rest assured that, just as fast as you
have grown, all of your stalks will crumble dry."

CAPITOLO VIII

O brighter than the day to me, and clearer,
O fortunate and glad and happy night,
hardly expected and therefore much dearer!

Stars, prompt and wise accomplices of Love,
you dimmed your luster, and the friendly dark
for me still tarried with no light above.

O timely sleep, leaving two lovers only
awake, while others you so much had won
that I could go invisible, unknown.

O kindly door, with so subdued and low
a sound were you then opened to me, that
he who was close could hardly hear or know.

O mind, uncertain if I dreamed or not
when by my goddess, oh, I felt embraced,
and this my mouth and hers became one knot.

'Twas you, O blessed hand, that led me next;
O quiet quiet steps preceding me,
O room in which I placed all of my trust.

O numberless embraces, with such countless
bonds you entwined our hips, our breasts, our necks,
fewer are those of ivy or acanthus.

To your ambrosia I, O mouth, returned,
ever unsated; O sweet tongue, O dew,
wherein I bathed my heart, so parched and burnt.

O breath, O giver of more pleasant scent
than among Indians or Sabaeans is
by some death-flaming phoenix ever lent.

O witness to my happiness, O bed,
bed, causing me to taste such a delight
I envy not the nectar of a god.

O bed, dispenser of my best rewards,
bed in the loving tussle more than once
ruffled and moved and shaken and disturbed.

I shall remember always, one by one,
all of you, causes of my high delight,
and ever praise you till my power be done.

Now it is time I mentioned, lamplight, you,
that, staying awake with us, allowed my eyes
fully to see the happiness I knew.

'Twas you, you only, doubled all that bliss:
no joy of love can be completely right
if we but live it by extinguished light.

Oh, how much sweeter in that act it is
to feed the glance now on her eyes divine,
now on her brow, now on her ivory breast;

to watch her lashes and her gold-curled hair,
and watch the roses scattered on her lips,
and with no fear of thorns put your mouth there;

to look upon her limbs which win and daze
all whiteness, and admit, while watching them,
God has bestowed upon them every grace;

and now indulge one sense, and now another,
till all of them partake of the same bliss,
with not a one left out in banishment!

Oh, why are, then, the fruits of love so rare?
Why is the time of all our joy so brief?
Oh, why so long and endless all our grief?

Why did you, envious Dawn, why did you then
desert your old Tithonus, ah, so soon,
bidding me, too, arise and quick be gone?

If only, being your foe, I could offend
and hurt you just as much! If your old man
now bores you, why not find a younger friend?

Oh, live, and let the whole world live in bliss!

Barbara Torelli (1475?-1533)

Born at Guastalla, this noblewoman married Ercole Benti-
voglio in 1491. In 1503, she met Ercole Strozza and fell in love
with him. The stormy scandal brought immediately a legal separ-
ation from her husband. In 1507 she married her lover, challenging the wrath of the Bentivoglios. The following year, Ercole
Strozza was slain.

Her famous sonnet, described by Carducci as one of the best
poems ever written by an Italian woman, starts with the conventional image of Cupid's dart and quiver, but redeems itself
at once through depth of pathos and height of feeling. The rest
of her *Rime* is sheer Petrarchism, though occasionally revealing
some terseness of expression.

ON THE MURDER OF HER HUSBAND

Spent is the torch of Love, broken his dart,
his quiver, and his bow, and all his power,
for cruel death has rooted out the bower
beneath whose tranquil shade I sweetly slept.
Ah, why can I not force the narrow tomb,
and still be with my love, and share his fate—
my gentle sire, who but five days and eight
could dwell with me before his boundless doom?

That gelid frost I'd thaw with all my fire,
and with my tears I would remold that dust,
and breathe new life on it with my desire.
Then, challenging, emboldened, to the one
who severed my dear bond, I so would boast:
"O murderer, Love has such a wonder done."

Michelangelo Buonarroti (1475-1564)

Born at Caprese, Michelangelo studied in Florence under Francesco Galeota, known as "the Greek." In 1488 he was apprenticed to Domenico Ghirlandaio. At fifteen he entered the Medici household where he came in contact with Lorenzo and the most brilliant humanists of his circle. The mausoleum of Pope Julius II, the Laurentian Library, the Medicean tombs, and the Sistine Chapel are the most significant milestones in the artistic career of this Renaissance titan, called "Divine Angel" by Ariosto. He met Vittoria Colonna and fell in love with her in 1547. He died in Rome and was buried in Santa Croce, Florence.

Like all poets, Michelangelo has a high and low tide of inspiration. He is least effective when he uses tools not his own, or re-echoes Dante's *Vita Nuova* or Petrarch's *Canzoniere*. His flame depends, then, on another flame; his images cannot take wing but are bound to the old imagery of Cupid's bow and arrows, of the phoenix and the salamander, and similar devices. But when he forgets arrows and bow, salamander and phoenix, his poetry is titanic, and he is once more the Michelangelo we know. This happens when his own heart becomes the subject of his poems and the fetters of imitation are broken loose by the hammer of his individuality. The expression may sound baroque but is not. Hammer and stone become the new, powerful image of Renaissance poetry, into which Michelangelo's soul enters not as song but as sense of Greek fate and Christian faith. His unmistakable force of vision and emotion is to the Renaissance what a sudden thunderstorm is to the monotony of a dry summer.*

* See my book, *The Complete Poems of Michelangelo* (The Humanities Press, 1969, 2nd edition) from which this selection has been taken.

I FEEL MORE PRECIOUS, I AM MORE
THAN ONE

I feel more precious, I am more than one,
for, since you held my heart, my worth grew more:
a marble block, when carving has been done,
is not the rough, cheap stone it was before.
As paper painted or just written on
no longer is a rag one can ignore,
so, since you aimed at me, and I was won,
my value's more, and no regret I bear.

Now, with your splendor printed on my face,
I go like one who, dressed with every kind
of amulet and arm, can dare all wars.
I walk upon the ocean, brave all blaze,
give in your name the light to all the blind,
and my saliva heals all poisonous sores.

ONLY WITH FIRE A SMITH CAN
SHAPE AND TAME

Only with fire a smith can shape and tame
his metal to the vision of his dream;
therefore no artist without fire refines
his gold and brings it to its highest gleam.
Nor can the wondrous phoenix, if not burnt,
resume its flight; if now ablaze I die,
I hope therefore to rise more bright with those
whom death makes great, and time can never dim.

Great luck indeed is mine that this same fire
should dwell within me still, quick to renew
one nearly in the number of the dead.
For, if by nature it can but aspire
to its own element, and I am, too,
now turned to fire, shall I be left behind?

HERE, TO MAKE SWORDS AND HELMETS, WAR DEVOURS

Here, to make swords and helmets, war devours
our chalices, and here Christ's blood is sold
by the quart, and cross and thorns are cast into mold
for shields and spears; and yet Christ's patience showers.
But let Him not return to this land of ours,
for here in Rome where sin is uncontrolled
His blood would spurt to the stars, His skin be sold
for any price in all streets at all hours.

The day I wanted to be poor, I came
right here to work: now one in his mantle does
what once Medusa in Mauritania did.
But if in heaven poverty and strife
are merits, what will ever mend our state
while other flags blot out the other life?

Finis

Your Michelagnolo in Turkey

SIMPLY BECAUSE THE SUN DOES NOT EMBRACE

Simply because the Sun does not embrace
with lucent arms this cold and humid globe,
they thought of calling night his other face,
that second sun they fail to know and probe.
Oh, but so frail is night that the quick blaze
of a small torch her very life can rend;
and such a fool is she, that the swift trace
of a gunshot can make her bleed and throb.

If something she must be, she doubtless is
the daughter of the sun and of the earth:
one gives her shade, the other holds her here.
But wrong are those who praise her qualities:
She is so dark, lost, lonesome, that the birth
of one small firefly can make war on her.

141

TO GIOVANNI, THE ONE FROM PISTOIA

I've developed a goitre in this chagrin,
as if I had, like cats in Lombardy,
drunk dirty water in large quantity—
which makes the stomach bulge up to the chin.
Beard to the stars, and a nape that I pin
upon the back, a harpy's breast—that's *me;*
and, dripping still, the brush, as you can see,
has made my face a floor stained out and in.

Into the belly have entered my hips,
and with the seat I counterpoise the hunch,
and, as I cannot look, in vain I go.
In front, my skin is taut and almost flips,
but in the back the wrinkles make a bunch,
and I am bent like an Assyrian bow.
That is why, bent and smirched
even my thought emerges from my head:
shooting a crooked harquebus is bad.
Defend my painting dead,
Giovanni, and my honor which grows fainter:
this place is bad; besides, I am no painter.

SINCE BY ITS SCENT I OFTEN KNOW
A STREET

Since by its scent I often know a street,
look, I have bought you at too dear a price
a little something smelling very sweet.
Now I shall always know, by this device,
wherever you may be, or we may meet.
I will forgive you if you hide your eyes
from me; but carry this, and I shall find
you easily, were I completely blind.

TO THE MARQUISE OF PESCARA

Turning, in restlessness, now right, now left,
I seek salvation's way.
Bewildered, between vice and virtue lost,
my heart is wearying me. I am like one
who does not see the sky
but goes from dark to darker path, astray.
I hand my paper, blank,
for all your sacred ink,
so love may undeceive me by the truth
piety writes upon it; so the soul,
detached from self, may not to error bend
my brief days left, and I may walk less blind.
Lady divine and high, of you I ask
whether in heaven a repented sinner
is less rewarded than a constant winner.

O NIGHT, O TIME OF SWEETNESS,
ALTHOUGH BLACK

O night, O time of sweetness, although black,
you give at last to all man's actions peace.
Who sings your praises, well he knows and sees,
and he who greets you feels no inner lack.
You cut and break all weary thoughts, which back
to us are sent by humid shade and breeze,
and from the lowest pit you lift with ease
of dream my longings to the highest peak,

and where I crave to go. O shadow of death,
halting all aches that rend both soul and heart,
O last and gentle solace of man's woes,
you heal our ailing flesh, restore our breath,
dry out our tears, lay all our toils apart,
and from the just you steal despair away.

THE GREATEST ARTIST HAS NO
SINGLE CONCEPT

The greatest artist has no single concept
which a rough marble block does not contain
already in its core: *that* can attain
only the hand that serves the intellect.
The evil I shun, the good that I expect
are thus, sweet lady haughty and divine,
hidden in you; but, to my utmost pain,
my art opposes its desired effect.

So Love is not to blame for all my woes,
nor is your beauty, nor indeed my lot,
if in your heart at the one time you bear
pity and death: it simply is because
my low intelligence, though burning-hot,
can only draw from you death and despair.

144

LINES BY GIOVANNI STROZZI ON THE "NIGHT" OF BUONARROTO

An Angel sculpted in this marble block
the Night you now see sleeping sweet and deep:
she is, therefore, alive, being asleep.
Don't you believe me? Wake her up: she'll talk.

ANSWER OF BUONARROTO

How good to sleep and—more—be marble block
while all about are harm and shame and woe!
Neither to see nor hear is my great luck;
so do not rouse me then, but please, speak low.

JUST AS AN EMPTY FORM

Just as an empty form
awaits its gold or silver liquefied,
and, broken, then, reveals
the perfect work; thus I can only fill
with inner life of love my void and need
of the immortal beauty of my lady,
both mind and heart of these my fragile days.
Through such a narrow space
her gentleness and love pour into me,
that, to draw forth her perfect image, I
must agonize and die.

IF MY ROUGH HAMMER GIVES A HUMAN FACE

If my rough hammer gives a human face
to this or that of all hard blocks that wait,
it is another smith makes me create,
controlling every motion, every pace.
But that divine one beyond stars and space
makes self, and others, with each stroke, more great
and bright; and since the first must generate
all hammers, *that* gives life to all, always.

And since the most effective is that blow
which falls from highest in the smithy, mine
shall fall no more—my hammer having flown.
Now here am I, unskilled, and do not know
how else to toil, unless the smith divine
shows me the way, who am on earth alone.

FROM HEAVEN HE CAME AND SAW
WITH MORTAL EYES

From heaven he came and saw with mortal eyes
the hell that stays, and that which shall not last,
then back he went to God in paradise
to give us glimpses of His splendor vast.
A lucent star, he shone above the vice
of that lost land which to me, too, was nest;
man's evil earth to him can be no prize:
God, You, who made him, can reward him best.

Dante I mean, whose works did not elate
that people, thankless and uncivilized,
who only to the just gives doom and hate.
Yet would that I were he! To be despised,
outcast, but born as he—for such a fate
I would give up the world and all things prized.

146

RESTLESS, CONFUSED, THE SOUL CAN ONLY SCAN

Restless, confused, the soul can only scan
some grievous sin committed long ago,
not recognized at all, but which you know
in your great pity on this wretched man.
I speak to you, O Lord: my every plan,
without your Blood, has brought mankind but woe.
Have mercy on me, born to serve your law,
revealing thus your bounty once again.

ENVOY

May I, who bore for years, carved in my heart,
the image of your face,
now that my death is close,
receive from love the privilege and grace
of having it engraved within my soul,
so that, serene and free, it soon may leave
the prison of its body. Only thus,
my lady, will my soul feel safe from harm,
bearing your image like a saving cross
through winds and storms and demons everywhere.
I shall take it to heaven,
whence Nature stole you on a happy day,
and give it back to all the angels fair,
so that they learn to make another face
as beautiful as yours,
and send a spirit down, wrapped in new flesh,
to keep the world, beyond your death, aware
of how divine and beautiful you were.

O MAKE ME SEE YOU, LORD, IN EVERY PLACE

O make me see you, Lord, in every place!
If mortal beauty burns me with its flame,
my fire is ember when at yours I aim,
and in your love I shall be still ablaze.
O dear my Lord, against my sad disgrace,
against my blindness I invoke your name:
for you alone can make me new, and tame
my longings, and uplift my mind so base.

You gave to time this soul, which is divine,
and in this weary flesh imprisoned it,
alas, to my regret and utmost pain.
What shall I do, no more to die and pine?
Without you, Lord, can come no benefit;
heaven alone can change the fate of men.

CERTAIN OF DEATH, NOT OF ITS MOMENT, I

Certain of death, not of its moment, I
know that a little life is left to me.
Friend to the senses, earth is enemy
to this my soul that urges me to die.
Blind is the world, and evil actions cry
victory over love and purity.
Dead is all light with its audacity;
outcast is truth, triumphant every lie.

When, Lord, will that thing come which men await
who still believe in you? Too much delay
severs our hope and keeps the soul in dread.
Why promise all your splendor on our night
if death comes sooner and makes all its prey,
catching us fallen, far from you, and dead?

RID OF A HEAVY, OVERBEARING WEIGHT

Rid of a heavy, overbearing weight,
and free, O Lord, from all this world at last,
to you I turn, a vessel from a vast
and fearful storm to where the calm is great.
Your thorns, your nails, and both your palms give fast
assurance that not long must I await
the grace that grants repentance for my past,
thus rescuing my soul from its grim fate.

Let not your holy eyes in judgment scan
my days that were; let not your ear, so long
offended, make you stretch an arm to fall
in anger on me. Let your blood wash all
my sins; let it more lavish be and strong
as I grow old. Quickly absolve my wrong.

ARRIVED ALREADY IS MY LIFE'S BRIEF COURSE

Arrived already is my life's brief course,
through a most stormy sea, in a frail bark,
at mankind's common port and at the shores
where one accounts for deeds both bright and dark.
I know now what a vain and faulty thing
my art has been, so far from its true source,
and how I made an idol and a king
of what man craves, but only brings remorse.

Of all my thoughts of love, once glad and vain,
what will now be, if to two deaths I'm close?
Of one I'm sure, the other threatens me.
No painting any more nor sculpture will
quiet the soul, turned to that Love divine
which opened arms, to take us, on the cross.

149

ANSWER OF BUONARROTO IN FRA BASTIANO'S NAME*

My lord, the hour your letter came to me,
about I went, seeking all Cardinals,
and gave at last your greetings to those three.

When to the major Medic of our ills
I showed your letter—well—he laughed so much
he shook upon his nose his spectacles.

Even the one you deem above reproach,
and like to serve all over, as you write,
was glad to read it, and has laughed as much.

The one who keeps the things most recondite
of our good minor Medic, I've not seen yet:
were he a priest, he too would have such right.

Others there are, who would deny, I bet,
Christ for your presence, more and more in demand
(the less they show their faith, the more they get).

Well, I will show your words to the whole band,
and if someone should find in it some fault—
O let him fall into the hangman's hand.

Monsignor Meat-still-seasoning-in-salt
(he also would be tender on the grate)
remembers you, more than himself, I'm told.

Our Buonarroto, who adores you greatly, having read your letter, seems to me
soaring a thousand times to heaven's gate.

The life of all his marbles, thus says he,
fails to bestow eternity on your name,
whereas your song divine makes *his* immortal be—

so great indeed that it is safe from harm
of cruel time or change of taste or fate:
true value cannot suffer death or blame.

As your dear friend and as my faithful mate,
he said: "Before my paintings people pause,
for his great verse, with votive candles lit.

"I feel myself a painter—one of those
which a rough painter with no skill nor worth
makes, mixing tubes and paints the way he knows.

"Thank Berni, then, the only man on earth
who understands me, but I think I can
assure him all my talent is a myth.

"But if I can his teaching's light obtain,
I'll make some day—a miracle indeed—
at least one worthy painting: a real man."

These things he told me. Now I must conclude
I cannot recommend this man enough,
who takes this present note for you to read.

While I am writing each new paragraph,
I blush, for I know well to whom it goes:
my verse is unprofessional, clumsy, rough.

No other news down here; so let me close
with my own fondest gratitude to you:
I am forever at your full disposal.

151

To you, who are a thing so rare and new,
I offer all myself, and this, as long
as I shall live, and still my hood goes through.

I say and swear that I would rather wrong
myself than you, my lord. I go in peace,
and ask your pardon for being a monk.

Command me, and do then whatever you please.

* See Berni's poem, "To Fra Bastiano del Piombo."

CAPITOLO

On the Collapse of His Body

I feel constrained and blocked as is the marrow
within its bone, right here, so poor and lonely,
or as some spirit in a vial narrow.

And my grave-dungeon is so small a flight,
Arachne dwelleth with her thousand clients,
all of them busy at their spinning task.

I have around the door mountains of giants:
those who eat grapes or take some medicine
go not elsewhere to place their putrid viands.

So I have learned to recognize the urine
and its emitting pipes: those many holes
still rouse me with their morning overturing.

Carcasses, cats, foul vessels, stinking bowls
for fertilizer, or just laid right there—
these are the things that greet whoever calls.

My soul would profit from my body, I swear,
for, should it come right out and smell this stench,
for bread and cheese it would no longer care.

My cough and cold, I gather, cannot quench it;
but, if they do, it must escape through the rear,
since through the mouth my breath can hardly venture.

Hernia, lumbago, lameness—oh, so weary
am I from all my work. Death is an inn
in which I live and eat the food I pay for.

Sheer melancholy is my joy within,
and my repose is but distress and trouble:
who wants all this—let hell soon grab him in!

153

All those Who at the Magi's feast are able
to see me must be brave, for this my house,
among such splendid palaces is rubble.

There's no flame left that still my heart could rouse;
if a great sorrow makes a small one dull,
its feathers plucked, my soul no more can rise.

I have a buzzing wasp within my skull,
and in a leather sack keep nerves and bones,
and three hard pills of pitch float in my gall.

My eyes are sand that has been ground of stones,
my teeth are keys of some old instrument
which make, when moving, jarring sounds and drones.

My face makes people scared and diffident:
to save the seeds, my clothes, without a stick,
would scatter every raven to the wind.

A spider in one ear has spun a thick
web; in the other sings a cricket all night;
no sleep, no snore, but a catarrhous trick.

Muses and love and all my drawings bright
are used to fold guitars, wrap meat for stews,
and to deck cesspools, brothels, with their sight.

To make so many puppets—what's the use,
if it has made me finish like the one
who crossed the sea and drowned in his own mucus?

Art, which I once have honored, and has done
me honor for some time, gives me such boon:
a poor old man who must serve everyone.

Ah, I am finished, if I don't die soon.

Baldassar Castiglione (1478-1529)

The famous author of *The Courtier* was himself a diligent, perfect courtier. He served, in various ambassadorial roles, the Montefeltros, the Della Roveres, and the Gonzagas. In 1524 he was sent on a delicate mission to Charles V by Pope Clement VII, who was later to blame the inability of his diplomacy for the infamous Sack of Rome of May 6, 1527—an unjust accusation which deeply afflicted him and, perhaps, even hastened his end. On hearing of Castiglione's death, Charles V was the first to mourn "one of the best cavaliers in the world."

Castiglione's poetic output is technically fastidious. He wrote four Canzoni in the Petrarchan fashion; ten sonnets, the sixth of which, reproduced in this Anthology, was often imitated but never surpassed; and a fifty-five-stanza "Ecloga" in which he succeeded in capturing some true echoes of Vergil.

O LOFTY HILLS, O RUINS RARE AND BLEST

O lofty hills, O ruins rare and blest,
where but the name of Rome is carven deep,
what wretched relics in your midst you keep
of souls once awesome, singular and best!
Theaters, arches by God's hand impressed,
colossal grandeur, glory's joyous leap,
you're now of ash and dust a little heap,
to passing throngs but mockery and jest.

Thus famous works that once on Time waged war
are felled, in turn, by the slow pace of Time
whose envy treads on names and deeds of yore.
But I will let no grief my spirit shake,
for, if time ends what is on earth sublime,
it, also, will perhaps annul my ache.

From THYRSIS' ECLOGUE

I

JOLAS.

When will it be that this my raucous lyre
will cease re-echoing my old lament?
Around these mountains either stone or briar
knows in what anguish all my life is spent,
and yet your cruelty has grown much higher,
O nymph, whose only joy is to torment,
for, if you hear of all my bitter smart,
deaf is your ear and merciless your heart.

II

Often, in view of my immense distress,
sheep do not feed their small lambs as before,
and, seeing their shepherd in such bitterness,
my young calves care to follow me no more.
At times, out of that wood's melodiousness
innocent birds have pity on my war,
and, often, hidden in their leafy shed,
they seem to sing my hope that is not dead.

III

You, you alone are worse than this old oak,
and harsher than the boulders in the sea;
you're more disdainful than a ruthless snake,
and beat a bear in bloody enmity.
No beast in all these woods my flock can shake
as you can bite my heart and all of me.
You're constant only in inflicting grief,
and, for the rest, you're mobile as a leaf.

IV

Well I remember when, along the brook,
for the first time I saw you plucking flowers.
'Twas then at me, my love, you deigned to look,
calling me your best shepherd at all hours.
You even said what bliss your spirit took
out of my song that moved all crags and towers.
A garland, then, around my brow you placed,
woven of privets and of roses chaste.

V

Alas, you snatched my heart out of my breast,
took it with you, that day, and have it still.
Since you won't make me with your presence blest,
what can I do if not be lost and ill?
No more of shady woods go I in quest,
nor do I care for lawn or lively rill.
I can no longer handle stick or rake,
and am no more the master of my flock.

VI

With weeping these my eyes have made a fountain
that can the thirst of countless people stop.
So come, you beasts, come down from that your mountain,
and drink with no more fear of net or trap.
And, fellow shepherds, though my eyes are fountain,
there's fire in my breast to warm you up.
Ah, every part and inch of this my soul
is now a flame that no one can control. . . .

X

Yet to their woods all beasts return each night,
where they forget their toil, and softly rest.
April comes back, and the new leaves are bright
in forests that were bare and snow-possessed.
Grapes in the fall grow black and ripe in sight,
and every fruitful tree brings forth its best:
only my grief cannot abate or cease,
only my anguish imitates no trees.

XI

But these dark days would surely limpid grow
if your cold heart were moved by pity's grace.
Fountain and woods would gurgle and would glow
if you, my nymph, were with me in this place.
With but sweet milk would all these rivers flow
if this my fire could all your coldness chase.
And my new verses would resound so sweet,
Linus and Orpheus would not dare compete. . . .

XVIII

THYRSIS.

God be with you, O shepherd kind and great,
who're venting here your flaming martyrdom.
So did your music all my longings sate,
for a long time I did not dare to come;
but the long road, that seemed my bitter fate,
for your sweet singing has so sweet become.
Now gladly this my weary flesh forgets
the trodden miles, their boredom, and their threats. . . .

XXIII

But tell me, Jolas, tell me if I, too,
am far from the one nymph I long to praise.
This, as a gift, I only beg of you,
and as reward for countless winding ways.
Oh, for one moment stop your song, in view
of the despair that in my question stays,
and help me find the one so dear to me,
if you're so gentle as you seem to be.

XXIV

So may your flock be safe forever more
from wolves and bears and other beasts that roam,
and may your lambs within their mothers' care
through a safe shortcut always come back home.
And so may this your lyre such music pour
throughout this mountain and this forest dome
that your fair Galatea soon may be
forever in your arms most joyously.

XXV

JOLAS.

For this your praise, so lavish and so strong,
how can I thank you, Thyrsis, dearest friend?
There are too many shepherds here, whose song
can make a stone in great compassion bend.
Boasting of my own verse would be quite wrong,
for it cannot, I know, so high ascend.
But, oh, there was a day when this my lyre,
which now can only weep, went high and higher.

XXVI

But if our goddess you so care to meet,
others, not I, will quench your burning thirst.
Not far from here, more shepherds you will greet,
who'll take you to her; I cannot, oh, first
because I never leave this lonely spot,
and then because there's sorrow in my breast.
Love keeps me company, and here, alone,
I hear cow, sheep, bird, rill, and echo moan.

XXVII

In the meantime, if you desire to rest
here in my cottage, I shall hold it dear.
Lie down, and slowly from your heavy chest
the burden of the road will disappear.
A quiet brook is here, the place is blest,
and a mild breeze is blowing, fresh and clear.
Chestnuts and walnuts, milk, and wine for you,
and—let me see—I have a cheesecake, too . .

Francesco Maria Molza (1489-1544)

Born in Modena, Molza spent most of his life in Rome. In his poem addressed to Sebastiano del Piombo, Francesco Berni referred to him as "a rascal." His rascalities, all in the realm of Venus, amused rather than shocked princes, cardinals, and popes. He was secretary first to Alessandro Farnese, then to Cardinal Ippolito de' Medici. He was a brilliant conversationalist, an extremely facile versifier, and an impenitent adventurer. After a long illness, caused by his effervescent eroticism, he returned to Modena where he had to win back the affection of his deserted family. He died in his native city. His Latin elegy, "To his Friends," which is the candid testament of both his life and art, has passages of deeply moving sincerity.

His "Ninfa Tiberina," which his contemporaries praised immensely, is a highly polished bit of Politianism, rather than Petrarchism, blended with elegant classical allusions. His *Stanze*, inspired by the portrait of beautiful Giulia Gonzaga, are in the Petrarchan fashion. But in his *Rime* there are flashes of inspiration and human interest.

ON THE RECOVERY OF HIS LADY

Like to a flower that on the humid earth,
all soaked with rain and bent by its own weight,
droops, and together with its scent, once great
and pleasant, sheds the color of its birth;
and neither youth nor damsel, held beneath
the yoke of Love in sweetness and delight,
waters it any more or keeps in sight,
seeing its primal glory come to death;

but if the sun with its new, pitying ray
comes to revive it in a tender fire,
quickly restored, it shares its splendor, gay:
so I your beauty, in this world so new,
have seen little by little disappear,
and then with greater grace return to you.

TO A YOUNG ITALIAN PRINCE

My lord, who at an age so young and green
often call Italy from her long sleep
so that again she may her glory reap,
whose majesty still makes your pity keen,
oh, on this sacred land that once was scene
and seat of kings, and now one bloodied heap,
look still, and let your bright escutcheon keep
her freedom as the noblest prize you glean.

And should Fate, mingled with man's blazing wrath,
to fair beginnings prove so hostile still
as to set evil traps against you too,
do not desist, my lord, from your great path:
never has Italy shown so strong a will
to fight and all her feats once more renew.

From LA NINFA TIBERINA

(I-V)

This lovely Nymph of mine, who, when she walks,
renders the Tiber more adorned and fair,
and when its banks are pale with icy rocks
still makes its current flow, with such despair
bids my enamored heart go where she goes,
I can but weep and laugh: oh, then and there
I find in her a thousand hidden graces,
in her fair soul a garden of fair roses.

Oh, were she not so heartless to me still,
and so fast fleeting from my love away,
behind those steps that these green banks fulfill,
my spirit, utterly content and gay,
and far above all needs of this my will,
would leap in joy and leave my dismal day.
Ah, but she comes and goes as fast as breath,
and brings my life to an untimely death.

Where'er she walk, where'er she turn her gaze,
April and May come with her at her whim,
for soon that vigor's back (to her, all praise!)
which gleams in every stalk and every stem:
so does the Sun, her brother, quickly raise
with but one glance the strength of night, grown dim:
but in the fair, bright showers that his light bring,
I've never seen so luminous a spring.

Nature seems to be playing with her thus,
and winds are vying but to hear her word,
and yet she never cared, and never does—
a wolf that even scorns to count a herd,
a stream ignoring banks through which it flows.
Little is she by lesser beauty stirred,
if ever at all: so glad and pure and gay,
she nothing needs but her own graceful way.

No freshness ever of nocturnal dew,
when the moon mantles in its silver light
and livens landscapes the sun almost slew,
and sacred forests once again makes bright,
can so restore the grass that begs a new
greenness from Jove, or so the shadow fight,
as one fair step or one clear glance obtains
of this my lady that within me reigns.

Teofilo Folengo (1491-1544)

The most original anti-classicist of the Renaissance, and a
precursor of Cervantes, Folengo was born near Mantua and en
tered, at the age of nine, the Benedictine monastery of Santa
Eufemia in Brescia. He studied philosophy at Padua and then
returned to Brescia. Probably in 1525, he obtained dispensation
from his religious vows and left the Order. He spent a few restless
years in Venice and Rome, where he was a tutor in several aristo
cratic families. But remorse, more than financial straits, made him
return to the monastic life of his youth, to which he was read
mitted after four years of probation and penance. He was sub
sequently sent to Palermo, and, later, to the monastery of Santa
Croce at Campese, near Bassano del Grappa, in the Venetian
region, where he died. Teofilo Folengo's stormy life was much
exaggerated by the impression of jollity and obscenity associated
with his literary works.

His poetic production is unique in the history of the Italian
Renaissance. To vent his rabid hatred of everything that passed
for classicism, he invented his own idiom—a language which he
called "macaronic" perhaps after the Northern-Italian "ma
caron" which means "noodles" and symbolizes the typical dish
of inns and taverns. In this peculiar language he blended Latin,
Tuscan, Lombard, and "cavaiolo," or Neapolitan, with the most
impeccable harmony of the Vergilian hexameter. The calm of his
parody is devastating. He ridicules the pomposity of the aristo-
crats, the corruption of the clergy, the insincerity of courts and
courtiers, the foolishness of poets with no poetry, and the manifold evils and injustices of his day. But underneath the boister-
ous laughter of his poetic world there is a deep feeling for the
suffering of such humble people as little old women working and
dying in poverty, poor simpletons robbed of a cow by unscrupulous gluttons wearing a religious cassock, and peasants oppressed
by fate and fellow men.

He called his Muse "Snoutine," and himself, "Merlìn Cocai."
His masterpiece is *Baldus*.

From *BALDUS*, Book VIII

Twenty or thirty "hoods" eat and devour Clarine.
One grabs a shoulder, one tears with his teeth the back,
one shouts for boneless meat, one wants to nibble on
the breast, another from the head eats off the eyes,
and from a well-cleaned bone one sucks the marrow out.
Have you perchance seen pigs around a muddy trough,
eager to drink and gulp their wishy-washy soup?
Thus poor Clarine is eaten by those monks who, when
Gypsy appears, invite to table their new guest,
and he accepts and starts to try his teeth at once.
To Butt he hands a bone adorned with little meat,
which soon he grabs, and swears he never ate so well.
You cannot hear a word: you only hear a noise
of broken bones, a wind of bellows on the soup,
for a big kettle, full of tripe, is boiling there.
They eat—and what a feast! Such as the Scriptures bid.
Already poor Clarine is short of legs and shoulders,
and now is laying bare her innards and great heart.
The more they eat, the more the hapless creature shrinks,
and cow and hunger fade at the same time away.
Reverend James is all trickling with oozing fat,
for only chunks of meat, not bones, he swallows down:
finishing up the sauce of several bowls, he licks
as dogs would lick, and sends from his deep chest big burps.
His belt he loosens now, and his big belly blooms,
and so he might well play upon that swollen drum.
His teeth work not at all, for he devours the meat
with opened jaws, and endless all his morsels are.
Fra Rocchus—look—is here, Fra Cad, Fra Antioch,
Fra Jasmine and Fra Dormouse and Fra Lazy-bones,
Fra Loaf, Fra With-no-head, Fra Stinking-all-the-time,
Fra Agathone, and Fra Arolfus, Fra Escape,
Fra Drunkard-twice, Fra Capon, Fra Broken-pants, Fra Line,
Fra Enoch. It is they give orders to the chef,
and have today made many masters of delight.

The stomach is their God, the soup their Law, a keg
their Testament. And now beneath the table lie
the clean smooth bones, and of Clarine there's nothing left.
Bones on the floor which dogs and cats will not dare touch.
Look, they begin to lick the fat on platters stuck,
and monks have never washed their dishes quite so clean.
Some of them scrape with clawy fingers the frozen lard,
some with their tunics' sleeves make every pot flash bright.
Feast over, they arise at last, and all play cards,
and then they fence, and then they often have a snack.
Such is the blessèd life these sacred people lead.
They always jest at men who from high pulpits shout,
who fast and flog themselves and bury those who die,
and who barefooted go, and write a thousand lies
in learned books in favor of Scotus or against.

'Tis evening. Gypsy wants to leave this place at once,
for at that table he has stuffed himself to death.
Butt grabs him from behind, and murmurs in his ear
that he should ask the monk to give him back his cow—
that monk (for he's the thief) his finger's pointing to.
So, laughing, Gypsy has a small sack brought to him,
in which he throws the bones beneath the table strewn,
and, placing it upon Butt's shoulders, says to him:
"Let's go, for in this sack you carry, Butt, Clarine.
Come on, we shall now both bury her in the ground,
and after but three days I'll make her rise for you."
This said, he bids farewell to all his jolly friends,
and starts to walk, with Butt coming behind, the sack
heavy upon his back. They reach a place at last
where from a ditch the frogs send to the stars their din.
And here the few remains of Saint Clarine are laid,
which great Cocaius deemed quite worthy of his song.

From *BALDUS*, Book XXV

And what was over there, that huge, enormous thing?
It was an empty dry pumpkin, which had been once,
In its green tender days, most edible indeed,
And could, no doubt, have made good soup for the whole world.
Functioning as a door, a spacious hole is seen
There at one side, through which Baldus the clown and all
The others enter. This is where the poets live,
Astrologers and singers, those who divine and write
Men's dreams and fill their books with empty foolish chat.
But listen to what pain each poet there is doomed;
Listen, astronomers, singers and chiromancers,
So that you, too, may stop concocting all your lies,
Which, through your art of parasites, please so your lords
Whom, as you wish, you make wonderful cullions of
By pouring into them your stuff of countless stars,
And calling things that are by porters understood
With but the common sense of what they see around them,
Precipitations of conjunctions in the skies,
Such as the one of Jove with Virgo and with Lion.
This pumpkin, empty, light, and so much like a bell,
Into whose emptiness dry seeds sound up and down,
Is the right dwelling-place for singers and for bards;
For, just as stone, hurled, must to the ground return,
Or fire which by itself soars to the fire supreme,
So light and futile things with one another blend.
Three thousand skillful barbers in this place you see,
Whose task—believe my words—is not to shave off beards,
But to uproot men's teeth with pincers from their jaws.
From Pluto they receive a stipend every year.
Quite frequently, alas, a singer, or a bard,
Or an astrologer, comes under each of them.
Each barber, while at work, stands high above a chair,
Holding between his legs the hapless culprit's head.

With horrid iron tools he loosens, first, the teeth,
and then with pincers pulls them out, deep roots and all:
and one at the same time can hear the endless screams
that travel to the sky in this unending deed.
It is high time they lost as many teeth each day
as are the lies they told upon the earth each day:
but oh, a tooth falls down and a new one buds forth!

And so, O my Snoutine, O greatest of the Nine,
I too, if you know not, must in this place remain,
no less entitled—I—to stay within this pumpkin
than he who makes Achilles, a humble Greek indeed,
better than mighty Hector, or even he who makes
Mr. Aeneas break Turnus's valiant chest,
and praises in his song a dandy much in love
with his own Phrygian cap upon his perfumed hair.
The pumpkin is my country: there I myself shall lose
as many teeth as are the lies in my great book.
Baldus, farewell: I leave you to those who do research.

. . . .

EPIGRAM

Down from the northern Alps the wicked wind returns,
    and with its bellows blows the forest leaves away.
Each river turns to glass, and to white lead each field,
    and everywhere the frost scatters its tapers. In
its shell the snail lies still, its horns completely hid,
    and the cicada dies of hunger, the fly of cold.
The little old woman sets a turnip on the table,
    but does not eat if, first, her spindle is not done.
The oily lamp makes still the pallid pedants wake;
    but, student, you have fun within so sad a night.

Vittoria Colonna (1492-1547)

Daughter of Fabrizio Colonna and Agnese di Montefeltro of the Dukes of Urbino, Vittoria Colonna was born at Marino, near Rome. Praised by Ariosto and loved by many artists and poets, she was the greatest literary attraction of her century. Her *Letters* give but a faint notion of the number and rank of the people with whom she came in contact. But she was as inaccessible as she was revered. After the death of her husband, Ferrante d'Avalos, Marquis of Pescara, which occurred a few months after the Battle of Pavia in 1525, she devoted her life to works of charity and lived in seclusion in various convents at Ischia, Orvieto, Viterbo, and Rome. She met Michelangelo in 1536. Their friendship grew into a deep and tender Platonic love, happily responsible for some of Michelangelo's greatest poems. Her *Canzoniere* makes of the Marquis of Pescara a far better man than he was in reality. In the second part it comprises poems of a mystical nature, full of theological complexities, at times so obscure and daring as to be frowned upon by the ecclesiastic authorities. Vittoria Colonna's fame is linked today more to Michelangelo's life than to her own poetry. Yet in some of her sonnets one can still see the reason for the immense reputation she enjoyed in her day.

From the CANZONIERE

1

A famished little bird, which sees and hears
the sounding of its mother's wings around
when nourishment she brings, in happy love
with food and her, chirps merrily, and cheers,
and struggles in its nest impatiently,
wishing to go behind her in her flight,
and, thanking her, in such a manner sings
that its tongue seems unwound beyond its might:

so I, whene'er the warm and lively ray
of that my sun divine, which feeds my heart,
flashes and more than ever dazzles bright,
urged by that love that lives within me, start
moving my pen, and thus his praise I write,
myself not knowing all the things I say.

2

Through bitter cliffs and rabid winds I'm knowing
in a frail bark the billows of this life.
And neither art nor mind have I for rowing,
and every aid to rescue me is slow.
Inclement death extinguished in one moment
him who to me was star and beacon bright;
against the raging sea and darkling heaven
no help have I—and greater grows my fright.

Not the sweet singing of a godless siren,
not the last crashing on these ruthless shores,
and not the sinking in the stormy sands;
but evermore the floating on this sea
which I have long and hopelessly called mine:
for death conceals my one true port from me.

3

O thought, in the high flight to which you spread
your pinions bold, no worth have I to climb,
so that to fail my task and burn my wings
would prove the end of glories still ahead.
With daring fancy so you kindle me,
I well agree to look on that fair light
which cannot die with my weak weary glance
losing in might while still alone you soar.

No wish have I to crave so great a dream,
for at its root my hope has been cut off,
and every pious star has turned malign.
Let my heart burn but never show a sign;
let my dismay, the worst of all, be hid:
soul, be at peace, and praise the holy light.

4

I only write to vent my inner sorrow
whereon my heart, which wants but this, is feeding,
and not to add to my fair sun new luster,
which left on earth such vestige of its glory.
And right am I in my desire for keening,
lest I should render his renown less shining:
with nobler pen and wiser saying, someone
will rise to save so great a name from dying.

Let blameless faith, and warmth, and grief intense
be my excuse with all; so deep are they
as to be curbed by neither time nor reason.
A bitter weeping, not an easeful singing,
darkness of sighing, not a limpid voice,
make me now boast of anguish—not of style.

5

I live upon this fearful lonely rock,
like to a bird that sorrowfully shuns
green boughs and waters clear; and from myself
and those I love on earth I stay apart,
so that my thoughts at once may reach the sun
I worship and adore. And though their wings
climb less than I desire, yet at my call
from other paths to this, turn they their flight.

And at the point they, glad and fervent, reach
the place I bid them to, their joy, so brief,
greatly surpasses any worldly bliss.
But if, obeying my full-kindled mind,
they could but glimpse the heaven of his face,
part of the Perfect Good would here be mine.

6

So many beauteous thoughts and high desires
were in me nourished by that Sun who chased
all clouds from everywhere, and brightened here
the day which now I see all over dark!
Within his brief stay on this earth he made
my sighing calm and all my weeping sweet,
for his wise word and his fair-shining glance
often could somewhat soothe my bitter smart.

His worth I see now spent, astray and dead
his lofty virtues, and the noblest minds
made by the common loss confused and sad.
Man's burning longing for the glories past
has from the world been banished with his death,
and bliss and I forever are apart.

Would that through living faith I full could see
with what great love God has created us,
and with what pain redeemed us, and with what
ingratitude we scorn so high a price;
and how he nurtures us; and how he grants
his treasures rich and rare with lavish hand;
and how he cares for sons in him reborn,
and more for those who more believe and love;

and how he in his great eternal sphere
kindles and arms a man with new desire,
when a strong warrior he promotes and crowns!
But since—the fault is mine—my lowly thought
to such a lofty height can never soar,
would I could know at least how he forgives!

Mid fog and frost I often run to God
for light and fire, so that my ice may thaw,
and this dark veil be opened and erased
by his supernal light and burning glow.
And though my mind be still in darkness cold,
yet all my thoughts are unto heaven turned;
and I within my heart's great silence seem
to hear a voice which but my soul can heed,

telling: "Fear not, for Jesus came on earth,
an ample ocean of eternal bliss,
to make all grievous burdens bearable.
Ever his waves more sweet and lustrous grow
to one who freely lets one's humble sail
to the deep bottom of his goodness go."

Now, Virgin chaste, from the fair ardent rays
of the true sun in heaven's bliss you live
your deathless day, who had a lofty place
on earth, where God's light lit your holy eyes.
As Man and God you saw Him then, when bright
spirits of heaven adorned your humble home
with limpid light and, timid all around,
in reverence stood, on their great task intent.

Immortal God concealed in mortal veil—
you worshiped Him as lord, reared Him as son,
loved Him as spouse, and honored Him as father.
Ask Him, therefore, to turn my saddened days
to mirth once more; and you, O Heavenly Lady,
show that you are in this desire a mother!

10

When will it be, O Lord, that, fixed on you,
my thought may gaze upon you evermore?
For, while it strays and wanders in the mist,
in the true splendor it can hardly pause.
Often I scan an image proud and fair,
foreshadowing your spirit in my heart;
and yet that lively hue, though flashing bright,
is never clear and shows itself in part.

Oh, let your wounded hand the veil now rend
that twenty years already in this blind
error has kept, and still is keeping me!
So that my soul, no more delayed by night
nor spurred by lustrous day, but all-unbound,
see the great sun in the most blessèd height.

Pietro Aretino (1492-1556)

The man who, after four centuries, is still known to the world as the "Scourge of Princes," was born in Arezzo, the illegitimate son of a shoemaker. He knew neither Latin nor Greek, yet, more than any other scholar, he represented and embodied the most diverse aspects of the Renaissance. He wrote comedies, tragedies, dialogues, "capitoli" in fluent terza rima, pornographic and religious sonnets, biographies of saints, threatening and affectionate letters, and in each of these fields he showed his colorful, versatile nature. With his *Pronostici*, a yearly almanac which he sent to princes, popes, and literati, he was a precursor of journalism. Called "divine" and "a miracle of Nature" by his contemporaries, he was the self-appointed "Secretary of the World." Of himself he wrote, "Every morning I divulge the praises and vituperations not of those whom I worship and hate, but of those who deserve to be worshiped and hated." But he hated more than he worshiped. A genius in the field of defamation, he made of his pen (he even boasted of his "armies of ink") a violent weapon against pedantry and pedants. Nothing and no one escaped the bitterness of his contumely. To have such a man, or, rather, such a pen on their side, was the desire of popes and potentates. Charles V of Spain invited him to ride next to him, and Francis I of France sent him a highly symbolic gift—a gold necklace, the links of which represented many little tongues. But this brilliant and unscrupulous adventurer of the word, who prized Ariosto's friendship, was intimate with Titian, and chose Fra Bastian del Piombo as godfather for his little daughter Adria, was also capable of much generosity. He helped needy widows and exigent orphans.

Aretino lived and ended his days laughing. As he was at table with his Venetian friends, in a sudden outburst of laughter he flung himself back in his chair, fell, banged his head on the floor, and died.

DIALOGUE BETWEEN A LOVER AND LOVE

"A man in love lives not,
nor does he die for love.
What is it, then, O Love, this mortal state?"
"An endless good and evil,
which nourishes all hearts on manna and poison."
"Who is it makes their difference be one
by varying his turns?"
"It is both fear and hope."
"Do you imply that, being with them both,
a fearing man lives not?"
"You clarify my thought."
"And one who hopes, dies not?" "You said it for me."
"If this is true, to what would you compare
a lover, half-alive?"
"To one who dreams of happiness and tears."
"True, for a man asleep is dead, yet lives."
"Such is a man in love."
"Who keeps us in such life and in such death?"
"Desire that burns in vain."
"Ruthless and pitying one, extinguish it!"
"Woe to myself and you, if I did that."
"Why, ever-changing god?"
"Ah, neither you nor I would then exist."

ON THE DEATH OF ARIOSTO

Ariosto, in this polished marble tomb
you sleep eternally, while your great name,
aware and glad of its own endless fame,
rises each morning with the sun in bloom.
But says your spirit from the firmament,
"What shall I do with such a lowly prize?"
Gazing on fulgent wreaths of starry skies,
oh, can you hear this lonesome, loud lament?

It is Apollo's sisters who still cry,
disconsolately saying, "Noble soul,
brighter than noonlight in a cloudless sky,
look on us orphans in our mourning dress
as, bent over your sepulcher, we keen,
and cast with every blossom our distress."

PRAYER

(1537)

Those eyes, O King of Heaven, which can make
every man happy and all angels blest,
oh, turn on mine, frozen and spent almost,
for I was, also, in your image made.
Those sacred hands, with which you, God, created
and then divided all the elements,
stretch on my limbs, so weak and anguish-weighted,
or teach my body to endure distress.

And with those feet, which sundered Pluto's gate,
and tread today on stars, oh, chase at once
far from my sight my ill and wicked fate.
Yet, if the end you have decreed has come,
let Death against me all his rights dictate;
but where you are, oh, deign that I come home.

Bernardo Tasso (1493-1569)

Torquato Tasso's father was born in Venice though his family came from Bergamo, Lombardy. He studied law at the University of Padua and, after serving several princes, was finally welcomed into the retinue of Ferrante of Sanseverino, Prince of Salerno, as his secretary. The catastrophic end of his lord marked the beginning of his financial straits. At the Court of Urbino he enjoyed the patronage of Guidobaldo II. He served, later, Luigi d'Este until, in 1563, Guglielmo Gonzaga of Mantua welcomed him to his court. He was elected Mayor of Ostiglia, where he died, bitterly mourned by his great son (see Torquato's "To the Metaurus").

He wrote two poems of epic length, the *Amadigi* and the *Floridante*. Of his various Eclogues, Psalms, and Odes, the latter have some technical importance in that they vaguely anticipate the metrical patterns of Parini's *Odes*.

COMPLAINT

The humble peasant, who has sown his seeds
    throughout his fertile field,
    and, with contentment sealed,
of bread is dreaming that already feeds
his children, fears no danger in his needs;

but if he sees, at harvest time, his land,
    whose fruit was soon to sate
    his little sons and mate,
suddenly seized and burnt by hostile hand,
and all his cherished hopes turned into sand;

or if he scans the horrid winter near,
    with skies outpouring snow
    and ice, and winds that blow,
unable to control his inner fear,
and only governed by his quick despair,

heaven he deafens with lament and cries
    for all the damage done
    cannot be now undone,
as it will take a sad, long year of sighs
to see the future lavish harvest rise;

yet in the presence of his faithful mate,
    and as he hears his small
    children around him call,
he calms himself, and can somehow forget
his bitter fate and its impending threat.

But I, who, like a daring seaman, went
  from sea to farther sea,
  with winds of perfidy
ever against me; I, who, battered, bent,
had safely come to port and merriment,

and was about to bind with anchor strong,
  and rope and other measure,
  my boat with all its treasure
so as to shelter it from any wrong
either of waves or some assaulting throng,

by unforeseen and sudden tempest I
  was thrown back to the ocean;
  by life's new gales in motion,
and by fierce pride that ever swells them high,
my boat once more was tossed 'mid waves and sky.

O billows of this false and wretched world!
  A wicked vortex vexed
  my life, broke my one nest,
and, granting me no peace or respite, hurled
my precious cargo with its fist unfurled.

Ah, but to make my days more dark and dreary,
  my Wife, the one and true
  column I ever knew,
the only solace in my grief and fear,
is absent, nor are my sweet children here:

under an alien sky, alas, they live!
  Who, therefore, will console
  this weary, worn-out soul?
Who, more than others, will some comfort give?
And who, if Death's inclement dart arrive

while in this grievous exile I am yet,
  who will be here with me
  in my last agony,
tenderly close these eyes, and sadly wet
with tears this face in its last calmness set?

And who, when I have said my last farewell
  to all the ended strife
  of this my wretched life,
will give me one last kiss, and softly call
my name during my lonely funeral?

Curb your relentless pride and cruelty,
  O rash and ruthless Fate!
  My strength is not so great
as Alp or wall or cliff, that I should be
still able to endure my misery.

Luigi Alamanni (1495-1556)

The most rabid anti-Medicean poet of the Renaissance, Alamanni was born in Florence. Involved in a conspiracy against Cardinal Giulio de' Medici, the future Clement VII, he had his property confiscated, and had to flee to France in 1522. Five years later, when the Medicis were ousted from Florence, he returned to his city which, in 1529, he defended bravely against Charles V. But in 1530 he had once more to flee to France where he sought and enjoyed the patronage of Francis I of Valois-Angoulème. To him he dedicated the two volumes of his *Opere Toscane*, in 1533. Resigned to the anguish of exile, he spent his last years in the comfort of poetry after several diplomatic missions to Italy which, though they gave him the joy of revisiting his fatherland, proved exacting and by no means conducive to literary *otia*. He died at Amboise, where Leonardo da Vinci had died in 1519. He wrote *La Coltivazione*, a poem in six Books in which he blended passages from Vergil's *Georgics* with lyrical details wholly his own; *Avarchide*, an epic poem in celebration of the city of Bourges; twelve Books of *Satires;* thirteen *Eclogues;* a comedy, entitled *Flora,* and *Liriche.* Alamanni brought to the poetry of the Renaissance the note of exile which had not been heard since Dante. In his book, *Un Exilé florentin à la Cour de France au XVIe Siècle*, Henri Hauvette rediscovered Alamanni's poetry and pointed out its influence, especially on Ronsard.

EXILE

The beauteous land, the place where I was born,
the fatherland I love, the flowered nest,
the dearest friends, the darling eyes I trust,
which made me weep yet did my song adorn,
I have to leave. Oh, why forevermore
was I the butt of fate's relentless wrath
when, wandering on this and on that path
to save at least my faith from cruel war,

to both myself and men I turned a foe?
But why still grieve? I should by now know well
how virtue in the world is dead and gone,
and how, when innocence is trampled on
and crime exalted, only those can dwell
gladly on earth whose guilt's their brightest show.

TO ITALY (1537)

I, too, can now return, may God be blest,
to see you, after six long years, again,
O my proud Italy—I who have lain,
because of foreign arms, far from your nest.
With reverent gaze, and tears that know no rest,
I sigh, and greet your first familiar slope;
but old despair and fright, and ire and hope,
still overwhelm this bliss within my breast.

The snowy Alps I soon will have to cross,
back to the Gallic land that more befriends
children of others than you do your own.
Within those shaded glens I'll build my house—
an ample home where I shall live alone—
if this is what you want and God allows.

186

TO THE SEINE

How much I envy you, O friendly Seine,
seeing your tranquil, joyous-gurgling waves
flow through fair fields and slake the summer thirst
of grass and flowers wherewith your banks are strewn!
The city that so curbs your mighty reign
you bathe and circle, and therein you see
how calm and how concordant those can be
who reap their joy from others' harm and pain.

But my fair Arno (God! Was there before
such anger gathered in so short a time
as I see fall upon it ruthlessly?) —
ah, my fair Arno in this raging war
is weeping, vanquished, all alone, and robbed
of its last ancient dream of liberty.

TO THE OCEAN

O Father Ocean, from the frozen North
you stretch your boundaries throughout the West,
and of the Gallic rivers take the best,
which Fate made subject to you on their birth.
May friendly winds and pure and limpid skies
breathe over you and clothe you night and day
whether you climb or downward wind your way,
so that your path be ever smooth and safe.

Oh, in our name, beg your much honored son,
beg the Tyrrhenian Sea to sleep no more
but to awake and to arise at last,
and feel some pity for the Arno bright,
who, old and full of woes and no more free,
is stagnant in his hopeless misery.

TO GOD

O highest, holy Maker, who are moving
both moon and sun with minor stars around,
and with a thousand other fair proud forms
are decking the whole world so copiously:
show us your mercy, show us now that day
destined to halt upon the Tuscan stream
its horrid storms, and let the joyous spring
of our new freedom once again return:

so that, in our own nest, we may once more,
who now are far and banished from all peace,
thank your great heart, so lavishly revealed;
and nevermore may all our godless foes
see us forever roam from shore to shore,
and, happy still, enjoy our harms and woes.

Francesco Berni (1497-1535)

Born in Lamporecchio of Valdinievole, Francesco Berni, called "Il Bernia" by his friends, studied in Florence. At the age of nineteen, to foster his ecclesiastic career, he went to Rome, "full of great hope," only to realize that Cardinal Bernardo Bibbiena, a distant relative, could not do much for him. In 1520, he served another Cardinal, Angelo Dovizi, nephew of the former prelate, and, later, was appointed Secretary to Giammatteo Giberti, Bishop of Verona. In 1532 he joined the retinue of Cardinal Ippolito de' Medici, who obtained for his new client and servant a lucrative position as Canon in the Metropolitan Curia of Florence, the very same that had once been held by Poliziano. In Florence he became the lively soul of all cultural and jolly gatherings, but, despite the joviality of his temperament, he was caught in the ferocious antagonism of Cardinal Ippolito and Duke Alessandro. Having refused to poison Cardinal Salviati, he was poisoned by Cardinal Cibo. Thus ended the life of the most brilliant anti-Petrarchist of the Renaissance.

His literary reputation was immense. Michelangelo in one of his poems said of him:

> . . . the life of all my marbles
> does not suffice to make your name eternal,
> whereas your song divine makes mine immortal.

But Berni had already called Michelangelo the sun of all the arts. In one of his "Capitoli" he had clearly stated that, in the midst of poets who could utter only polished words, Michelangelo alone expressed ideas. Berni's anti-Petrarchism found its most effective voice in the "capitolo," a new form of realistic, caustic, effervescent satire, known today as "Bernesque."

TO FRA BASTIANO DEL PIOMBO*

Father, to me more reverend than those
who have the title of "Most Reverend"
and whose high reverence no person knows;

good Father, reputation, ornament
of friars that have been and that will be,
including all those Jesuits dull and bent;

how have you been all this long time? And he
who is no woman yet we love so much—
how is the one who stole my heart and me?

Michel'Agnolo Buonarroti is such
that, when I see him, I would gladly light
candles to him, burn incense as in church;

and this, I feel, would be both good and right,
better, that is, than wearing, to thank God
for health regained, a garment red or white.

I think he really is, just as he should,
the idea of sculpture and of architecture,
as Mona Astraea, of justice. And I add

that, should one make a statue, or a picture,
of both these arts, one would but choose that man
as model: there's no other thing in Nature.

You know yourself his merits—how he can
judge, think, with wisdom and with great discretion,
and how good, truth, and beauty are his plan.

I saw a couple of his compositions
and, though I'm ignorant, I want to say
I read them all in Plato's high conceptions.

Apollo and Apelles live today.
Enough of you, O pallid violets,
and liquid crystals, nimble beasts astray:

you babble words but he, instead, says thoughts.
So, modern chiselers, and even old,
go, all of you, to the sun and take notes.

All, except you, of those who are so bold,
reverend Father, as to try your trade
should to the women have their colors sold:

for you alone, and rightly so, indeed,
can be quite close to him, so as to know
how rare and perfect friendship here is made.

To save him from old age and all its woe,
we should now find the cauldron where, one day,
Medea fried and fried her father-in-law.

Would that Ulysses' wife still lived today!
She would make you and him so young again,
you would outlive Tithonus I should say.

It is dishonest and it gives me pain
to think you, who make stone and wood alive,
will have to die like asses dull and plain,

while oaks and olive trees will, ah, survive
with crows and ravens, dogs of any kind,
and countless far worse beasts that should not live.

But this my reasoning is vain and blind—
so I shall stop, or they will say that we
are Lutherans or Mamelukes in mind.

Humbly I beg you, Father dear, to see
that I'm remembered by my Agnolo,
and that with kindness he still thinks of me.

And, also, if you think the Pope should know,
tell him that, here, I praise him and adore him
as Master and Christ's Vicar. When you go

to consistory, all Cardinals before him
you'll see, I hope: to three of them go close,
give them my best and of my love assure them:

who the three are, your intuition knows.
Don't tell me now: "You pest!" You know too well
how in that place each ceremony goes.

Monsignor Carnesecchi you will tell
I do not envy what he has to write
nor those who to his ears are bothering bell.

But I remember the fried squash I ate
last year with him; its beauty—tell him this—
my gluttonous glances still can contemplate.

And, Father, give my love to one I miss—
to that big virtuous rascal, Molza dear,
who has become, toward guiltless me, remiss.

Without him, I have lost an arm, I fear;
I write to him each day, then I destroy
my notes which are plebeian and not clear.

Ask him to tell his Master that my joy
will be to serve him from now on, both far
and near, and that his grace I most enjoy.

Be well, and don't work hard, even if you are
tempted to paint each charming face you see:
O my sweet Father Bastian, take good care!

In Ostia, then, as soon as it may be.

* See Michelangelo's poem, "Answer of Buonarroto in Fra Bastiano's Name."

MARRIED LIFE

A meager roast of birds, whiche'er they are,
or salty meat without one sip of wine;
to find, when tired, no chair where to recline,
or have the fireplace near, the bottle far;
to pay today and hope to save each dime,
to lend your cash, a creditor to be;
to join a feast and nothing there to see,
and sweat in winter as in summertime;

to have a tiny pebble in your shoe,
and in your stocking feel a fleeting flea
like a quick courier shuttling to and fro;
to have one hand quite dirty, one quite clean,
and show one leg full-covered, one all bare;
to be in a great haste, and have to wait:

add more if more is there,
and number every spite and every strife:
but the worst evil is to have a wife.

THE BEAUTY OF HIS LADY

A hair of tenuous silver, stiff, entangled,
artlessly round a graceful face of gold;
a waving brow (I gaze, and soon grow pale)
upon which Love and Death blunt all their darts;
wandering eyes of pearl, and glances twisted
from all unequal things in front of them;
lashes of snow, and hands and fingers short
and sweetly stubby (how they make me smart!) ;

two lips of milk, a wide celestial mouth;
ebony teeth half there, half gone astray;
a sweet, unheard-of harmony from heaven;
behavior proud and heavy: O divine
servants of Love, to you this man confesses
such is the beauty that my love possesses.

THE BEARD OF DOMENICO D'ANCONA

Can anyone on earth be, ah, so stony
as not to mourn with burning eyes and leaping,
filling the sky with sneezing and with weeping,
the beard that was Domenico d'Ancona?
What thing is ever of such worth and beauty,
which envy, time, or death, does not annul,
or who will rise to save it from them all,
if man's relentless hand reaps, too, its booty?

Now you have thrust, O barber, your last blows
on the most singular of all men's beards
that ever were described in verse or prose.
Better it would have been to cut his neck
than to shave off so beautiful a thing
as could have been enbalmed, and then laid there,
among all wonders rare,
in full perspective on an entrance door
to keep his image on this earth alive.
But let me now at least
remember this disaster of dark hues,
serving as epitaph upon a stone:
"O tragic case to mourn, ah:
here lies the crowning glory of all beards,
which once was of Domenico d'Ancona."

His Holiness does nothing else but eat,
His Holiness does nothing else but sleep:
this is the news that those around him keep
telling the anxious crowd down in the street.
His speech, his vision, his complexion's good;
clean tongue, good breathing, clear expectoration:
all these are signs of physical duration,
and yet his doctors swear that die he should.

Their reputation crumbles if the Pope
stubbornly comes out of their hands alive,
for they have warned, "He's finished; there's no hope."
Dismal old symptoms, complications new:
"He had a seizure yesterday at two,
and one today, and by next dawn no other."

They would be glad to slaughter
a dog, not just the Pope: but so they'll try,
in spite of everyone they'll make him die.

THE PONTIFICATE OF CLEMENT VII

Pontificate replete with kindly thought
and many a speech and more consideration;
full of "then," "if," "perhaps," in a gradation
of words and empty words, and nothing but;
consisting of ideas and dear advice,
of guesses much too thin to shake the nation,
and (bring your purse along!) of invitation
to audiences, so witty and so nice;

of leaden feet and firm neutrality,
of patience and of many a goodly show
of faith and even hope and charity;
of innocence and sweet intents that glow
and mean, in other words, simplicity,
if you still care to call them kindly so.

Oh, bear with me, my foe:
I still maintain, little by little he
will canonize Pope Hadrian, you'll see.

SIR CECCO AND THE COURT

Sir Cecco cannot live without the Court,
nor can the Court survive without Sir Cecco.
Sir Cecco only needs one thing—the Court,
and so the Court has but one need—Sir Cecco.
Let those who care to know about Sir Cecco
ponder and grasp the meaning of the Court:
this our Sir Cecco is quite like the Court,
and this our Court exactly like Sir Cecco.

Upon this earth is bound to be the Court
as long as life remains in our Sir Cecco,
for they are one, Sir Cecco and the Court.
If in the street you ever meet Sir Cecco,
you can be sure you'll also meet the Court,
for, arm in arm, the Court walks with Sir Cecco.

May God protect Sir Cecco,
for, should he die through error of the Court,
they're ruined both, Sir Cecco and the Court.
But if he dies, at least
this fortune will console the human race:
Trifonè will continue in his place.

Giovanni Guidiccioni (1500-1541)

Among ecclesiastics called by Carducci "essayers of beds and ther things," Guidiccioni was truly pious and devoted to the ause of charity. In favor of the poor, or "Straccioni," he wrote is famous Oration which he addressed to the Republic of Lucca, is native city. A student of jurisprudence, he was close to Carinal Farnese. When the latter became Pope Paul III, Guidiccioni ras made Governor of Rome and Bishop of Fossombrone. While 'apal Nuncio to Spain, he was accused of treason against the Ioly See, but his innocence triumphed and the Pope appointed im President of Romagna in 1539. In the last year of his life e was Commissioner of War (against Ascanio Colonna), and iovernor of Ancona. Recent scholarship has proved that he died f natural causes, and not, as had been suspected, of poison.

His *Canzoniere,* a lucid tribute to Petrarch, has in some of ts madrigals a felicitous breath of poetry; but it is his two onnets, "To Italy," that keep his fame alive.

TO ITALY

I

O worthy foster mother of bright nations,
in less dread days triumphant in the world,
once a serene and bright abode of gods,
now home of tears and mournful implorations:
how can I hear the sound of your lament,
or watch, without deep sorrow rending me,
your lofty empire sunk into the sea,
and so much glory, so much honor, spent?

Ah, though a slave, such regal grace you bear,
and so your name resounds in this my heart,
I kneel, and kiss your remnants everywhere.
How did one feel who saw you in your might,
splendidly seated in your throne of light,
a diadem of gold around your hair?

II

Oh, from the sleep and from the heavy sloth
in which, my Italy, you long have lain,
now rise, and breathe, and number with disdain
all of your wounds, O fool and servant both!
For the fair freedom which in maddened deeds
you lost to other nations, sigh and yearn,
and from the wicked to the righteous path,
you, who're about to stray, your steps now turn!

For, if you think upon your ancient days,
you see that those who made your triumphs bright
have now enchained you underneath their yoke.
Your foul desires, by which you are oppressed,
have brought you to this end, and have become
your bitter harm and others' boastful jest.

MADRIGALS

I

When down within my heart
your gentle voice resounds
 (I give thee thanks, O Love) ,
no longer do my torments make me smart.
But when I lift mine eyes to gaze on those
far brighter stars than mortal heaven shows,
such is the bliss that floods my heart that I
neither for life nor freedom want to sigh:
and should I die in such a blissful rest,
nobody's life would be, as my death, blest.

II

O graceful, limpid pearl,
that with the splendor of your ardent ray
lend luster to all men,
and take all glory from the sun away,
oh, listen to the words I have to say.

I say that when you came
into this world, the stars,
happy and gay and fair
in Love's most clement heaven were aflame,
and never had Admetus' tiny shepherd
shown us a kinder day.
The air, the land and sea,
were seen to smile, and the lascivious breeze
to play with blossoms and with grasses green.
Nor did the birds forget
to mention then your name: in flocks, flocks new,
they with their singing made a joyous Spring.
Oh, why can I not sing
your praises, just as I would like to do?

Giovanni Della Casa (1503-1556)

Born at La Casa in the Mugello, Florence, Giovanni del
Casa is the internationally famous author of *Galateo*, a book o
good manners, the importance of which lies not in its conten
but in its style. A highly erudite ecclesiast (he studied at B
logna, Florence, and Padua), his career did not end with tl
Cardinal's hat which he desired almost immoderately—he ha
already been Archbishop of Benevento, Papal Nuncio to Venic
and Secretary of State to Pope Paul IV. In Latin he wrote
biography of Pietro Bembo and a treatise on the advantag
and disadvantages of married life. As a poet, he was hailed a
an innovator of the sonnet, to which he brought a freer relea
by breaking the rigidity of its cadences and carrying into tl
next line or quatrain a thought or a sound expected to fall els
where. But not in this are we to see Della Casa's important co
tribution to Italian poetry. He has, as in the sonnets "To a Forest
and "To Sleep," a voice of unusual sincerity and a depth o
poetic feeling unknown to most Petrarchists.

TO A FOREST

O solitary tranquil forest, friend
to these my thoughts, much wearied and dismayed,
while Boreas on turbid, shortened days
ruffles both air and earth with horrid frost,
and while your verdant, ancient, shady hair
seems, just like mine, all over to have grayed,
now that, instead of blossoms white and red,
your every open place has snow and ice,

on this so brief and nebulous a light
still left to me I muse, and I feel, too,
an icy numbness over flesh and soul.
But, in and out, I freeze much more than you:
a harsher Northwind will my winter bring,
with colder, shorter days, and longer night.

TO SLEEP

O Sleep, O peaceful son of quiet, dark,
and humid night, O comfort of us weary
mortals, O sweet oblivion of all grievous
evils that make life boredom and distress;
succor at last this heart that languishes,
and finds no rest, and soothe these frail and tired
limbs; fly to me, O Sleep, and over me
fold your black wings, and halt right here your flight.

Where's silence, which abhors both day and light?
And the thin slumbers that with doubting feet
are wont to tread behind you, where are they?
Ah, that in vain I call you, and in vain
I try to lure these dark cold shadows. O
my bed of harshness! Hard and bitter nights!

ON THE PORTRAIT OF HIS LADY,
PAINTED BY TITIAN

Titian, how well I see my goddess beam
in features new! On your live canvas she
opens and turns her beauteous eyes, and speaks
and truly breathes, and moves each gentle limb.
O joy! My heart a double comfort finds,
which makes it often sigh; and while it looks
now on this face, and now on that, it seeks
the truer one—and where, it does not know.

But how, how can I ever try to forge
of this high image the eternal part—
a dull smith chosen for a task so bright?
Since Love, O Phoebus, makes me fond of it,
you, raise my style, so that such subject might
bring endless glory to your noble art.

ON THE SAME SUBJECT

Is this, O Love, the graceful golden hair
amid white milk and dewy roses cast,
which I would seize, and so avenge in part
the deep and smarting wounds I have to bear?
Is this the lofty brow that hides that will
which, as it pleases, rules my every wish?
Are these the eyes whence all your arrows start,
which could from nowhere else shoot forth so strong?

Who on so small a cloth drew the fair face
which, ah, my verse still tries in vain to paint?
Myself for this, and art itself, I blame.
Here we are watching the new miracle,
born on the Adriatic Sea, whereby
Goddesses are reborn, and keep their fame.

JEALOUSY

O Care, who feed and grow on fear alone,
and grow much stronger just by fearing more,
and, while your ice with flames you mix and pour,
perturb and sadden the whole realm of Love:
since in an hour you've poisoned my delight
with all your bitterness, leave quick my heart,
go back to Hades, to the tearful, sad,
infernal fields; there, to yourself be foe,

and there, spend all your days with no rest ever,
your nights with no sleep ever, and be there
oppressed by certain and uncertain pain.
Away! Why, fiercer than you're wont to be,
now that your poison runs through every vein,
with still more wraiths do you fly back to me?

TO THE VENETIANS

These palaces and balconies, adorned
with purple marbles and with carvings bright,
were once a few low houses closely built,
deserted shores, and islets quite forlorn.
But valiant people, of all vices free,
were crossing with small sails the ample seas—
people who, not to tame more provinces
came here, but to escape from slavery.

By no ambition were their hearts made bold,
and more than death did they abhor deceit,
nor were they ruled by ravenous greed for gold.
Though heaven grants you a more blessèd fate,
those ancient virtues, which I most admire,
by your new wealth are buried and annulled.

TO GOD

This mortal life which, dark and cold, expires
in one or in two brief nocturnal hours,
has heretofore involved in its bleak clouds
the nobler part of me. But now I turn
to gaze upon your graces manifold;
for fruits and blossoms, summer heat and ice,
and such sweet laws and measures of the skies,
teach me about you, O eternal God.

This now so limpid air, and this clear light,
which opens universes to our eyes,
'twas You who raised from chasms vague and dark;
and all that shines in heaven or on earth
was locked in shadows, and you opened it;
for day and sun are but your handiwork.

Annibal Caro (1507-1566)

Born in Civitanova, Annibal Caro studied at the University of Florence. In Rome, he won the patronage of Pier Luigi Farnese and, later, of his sons, Ottavio and Cardinal Alessandro. His fame rests mainly on his verse translation of the *Aeneid,* still unsurpassed, and on his *Letters,* not inferior to Tasso's for vividness of emotion and elegance of style. He was, after Bembo, the most impeccable prose writer of the Renaissance; his critical judgment was respected by poets and artists. In the last years of his life he was dear to Michelangelo. His *Canzoniere* contains poems of exquisite terseness. The following "Song to Flying Time" is, I believe, the best of Caro's poetic production.

SONG TO FLYING TIME

Alas, how fleet and light
this life you love so much,
speeding to its own end, goes headlong down!
Down from a mountain's height
no weighty rock with such
velocity or haste is ever blown;
nor does an arrow, thrown
by hand of valiant might,
leave with such speed its bow
as life is seen to go,
hiding its very going from our sight:
so forceful and so fast
that if a day dawns bright, another's passed.

O clear and tranquil stream,
while in your crystal bed
I mirror all myself, you make me see
the greedy face of Time—
Time that, before he's fled,
has stolen with my youth the best of me.
Farewell, fair company,
O season of delight!
Those days of blissful sigh
down to their roots are dry.
The features that were young are marked with night,
and soon I have to bear
old age and still more gray and thinning hair.

Sweet life, so dear to me,
if you can please men so,
why do you fly so fast, leaving, instead,
a bitter memory
of all your passing glow?
Why can you not come back, once more to feed
on air, our only food?
At least a stream retains
its form in all its motion

though still its current runs,
morning and evening, swiftly to the ocean;
but, life, forevermore
you leave with all our days our human shore.

Poor wretches that we are!
In empty hopes the fire
of all our longings in a while is lost,
and oftentimes too far
are we by passion dire
driven away and into ruin thrust!
Sure of one day, what must
man call his own, if so
rapidly, life, you run?
Quickly destroyed and done,
the soul so feels the sharpness of his claw
as does a weary horse
spurred on too steep a slope along its course.

If this our fate is willed
by the unchanging stars—
that our existence should such laws obey—,
is there a fairer shield
against inclement scars
than deed of beauty or creative play?
Time threatens our one day
with its eternal woes:
so let's our hours make bright,
and with deceit of light
lessen or shun the darkness of his blows.
Thus can we conquer all,
and only with this hope fear not our fall.

Therefore, my soul, unfold
your Heaven-granted wings,
and fly away from your accustomed fears!
By hope and faith made bold,
with what their firmness brings
you'll know at last the happy-ringing spheres.

But, first, oh, shun the snares
of man's insane desire,
or never will you climb:
for once, in youthful time,
nature it was that gave you easy fire.
Passion in youth can win,
but in old age it's only grievous sin.

While sunshine floods the east,
a carefree pilgrim goes
gathering buds and blossoms off his path;
but when the sun's deceased,
long shadows are his foes,
and if he leaves his road, he faces wrath
and darkness, and the death
of forest, thick and bare,
without one saving nest.
Thoughtful is he, and blest,
who, having strayed beyond his senses' snare,
returns on his old road
and finds in his last years God's safe abode!

So with these thoughts I wait
for my delightful rest,
here in this place; and may I here remain
long in this tranquil state,
by no more cares oppressed,
and sheltered by this river's fresh domain.
And may I now obtain
 (fate seems to heed my plea)
that, as I older grow,
I may fair weather know
despite the storms that fight my flesh and me.
And may this final sky
stay unperturbed if for my past I sigh.

My Song, you are not such that you should hope
still to endure the war
of greedy Time that wins forevermore.

TO GOD

Ill and so full of years and, more, of sins,
now lies your servant, Lord; and the double burden
of two deaths crushes him, who came at once
so close to both, and sighs, and is afraid.
One would, indeed, be sweet and dear to me,
who, dying, would be ridden of such weight;
but ah, the other horrid step! Let first
my tears and then your blood cleanse all of me!

Oh no, not life, O Lord—I want but time
to die in grace. And since I am allowed
to hope for this, for You are good and I
repent, I see salvation in your glory,
and come to You at last, content to die,
at peace with man, forgetful of all worry.

Angelo Di Costanzo (1507-1591)

Better known for his *History of the Kingdom of Naples,*
which goes from 1250 to 1486, Di Costanzo published a most
successful *Canzoniere* in both Latin and Italian. His contemporaries admired, and even imitated, the sheer element of surprise
which concludes most of his sonnets.

Born in Naples, he cherished Sannazaro's friendship. Like
many other poets and artists, he fell in love with Vittoria
Colonna. In 1546 Don Pedro of Toledo, Viceroy of Naples, exiled
him to the Castle of Cantalupo where he spent three years of
bitter, though intellectually fruitful, solitude. Back in Naples, he
was an influential member of several learned academies, and,
in 1589, at the age of eighty-two, was a magistrate of the
Neapolitan Court. He died in Naples.

We can still admire the freshness and sincerity of some of his
sonnets. After Alamanni and Di Tarsia, he expressed the sorrows
of exile with the most unforgettable music.

EXILE

Here, on the Regal Alps' opposite part
where Boreas and winter are so strong
that I can hear not even one bird's song,
and see upon the hills not one leaf start,
I moan my grievous exile and the joys
of my life crumbled and my hopes all spent,
and ever call the cause of my lament,
and there is none replying to my voice.

In so much grief one comfort I can find,
which, in whatever place I'm sorrow-strayed,
restrains my soul from its desire to die:
there is no dell or solitary shore
where upon bark or on the sand or stone
Love does not paint her face before my own.

TO HIS CHILD

Like to a dove immaculate and pure,
alas, you flew so suddenly to God,
O blessèd soul, and left me blinded here
within this valley dark with pain and woe.
But if some fondness still remains in you
of the dear father you so loved on earth,
and who beneath the sky can nothing find
that might console him in his dismal dearth:

when during sleep, brother to death no more,
my saddened spirit, buried in its grief,
to all the other senses shuts the door,
send me, sometime, from the fair Milky Way
at least your shadow, that may comfort me,
swaddled within your glory's limpid ray.

THE DEATH OF VERGIL

O happy swans, who guard the Mincius blest
and all its waves and banks, in Heaven's name
oh, tell me now the truth of the old claim:
was our great Vergil born within your nest?
And you, fair Siren, where in tranquil rest
and easeful joy he loved to spend his day
(and may his bones be calm forever!), say:
are his remains now truly on your breast?

What greater grace from Fortune could he have,
what other end so like his very birth?
Was not his cradle fully like his grave?
Born in the music marvelous and sad
of white white swans, now that he is no more,
he's ever mourned by Sirens darkly clad.

TO VITTORIA COLONNA

The sea will sooner lose its fish and waves,
the sky all of its stars, the air its winds,
the sun its lucent and life-bringing rays,
and the earth tender leaves and grass in May,
than I, though turning face and step elsewhere,
shall, O my soul, remember you no more,
and no more seek with all my sighs ablaze
only your beauty, first of all that's fair.

A futile error makes you think, therefore,
that I may leave to shun this fire I feel,
or I may long to die of alien wound.
For, though no torment be as harsh as mine,
I'd rather shed this life for you than share
or find my bliss in anything less fair.

WISHING TO DIE, WITH MANY ENTREATING RHYMES

Wishing to die, with many entreating rhymes
I have been calling Death a cruel foe,
for never prompt was he to rid my life,
chargèd with anguish, of its wrath and woe.
But now that softer and more fertile breeze
is blowing for the sailing of my ship,
now I love life, and still entreat my Fate
to grant me not a sad but happy trip.

Lovers, be joyous in your hapless love,
for many a time the gentlest bliss is born
from some unheard-of smart, some grievous pain.
Fortune and Heaven often change their style:
I see in winter those clear days and blooms
which rain and thunder in their April dooms.

WHEN WE SHALL BOTH HAVE CROSSED THE DARKENED WAVES

When we shall both have crossed the darkened waves
of the black Styx, and hopelessly shall be
condemned to dwell upon the scorching sands
of the infernal, deep, abysmal caves,
then shall I hope my utter misery
would turn to joy and utter happiness
were I to see your calm and limpid eyes
which now disdainful pride conceals from me.

And, watching my unprecedented woe,
you then would ease the smarting of your pain
with your rejoicing in my final blow.
But, ah, I fear that, for our new disgraces—
you loved too little, and I loved too much—
we'll have the selfsame doom, but different places.

Luigi Tansillo (1510-1568)

Born at Venosa, the little town between Apulia and Lucania which Horace has made famous with his song, Tansillo spent his childhood in Naples. He started and finished his courtly career in the service of Viceroy Don Pedro of Toledo, with whom he traveled extensively inside and outside of Italy. After the death of his munificent patron, he returned to Naples, and died at Teano after a few anticlimactic years as "Captain of Justice" of Gaeta.

He started his literary career with the publication of *I Due Pellegrini*, an eclogue which revealed his poetic fervor. In 1532 his new poem, *Il Vendemmiatore*, full of brilliant passages and rich in sensual overtones, deeply displeased the Pope. To placate his censors he wrote *Le Lagrime di San Pierto, (The Tears of Saint Peter)*, a book which was to start that pietistic "literature of tears" so abundant during the years of the Counter-Reformation. An elegant Petrarchist in his *Rime*, he was also aware of other literary fashions. His *Capitoli* are Bernesque in spirit, and his *Podere* is Vergilian in tone.

The sonnet, *"Poi che spiegat'ho l'ale al bel disio,"* which we find included in Giordano Bruno's *Eroici Furori*, was attributed by some critics to the philosopher of Nola; but it was published with the name of Tansillo in the Ruscelli Anthology of 1558, when Giordano Bruno was only a ten-year-old schoolboy.

THE FLIGHT

I

My wings are fledged by Love: therefore so high
my daring mind unfolds them that I hope,
higher and higher soaring, to renew
man's war against the portals of the sky.
If I look down, I dread my flight's great height;
but, proud, he shouts and reassures me then
that, if from my bright course I fall and die,
timeless is fame, and mortal but my leap.

For if another, spurred by such desire,
gave, dying, to the sea his deathless name
when the sun severed all his pinions bold,
this, of you too, the world will have to say:
"He tried to reach the stars, and if he failed,
not his audacity—his life gave way."

II

Now that toward beauty I have spread my wings,
the more I see the air beneath my feet
the higher to the wind my proud wings fly,
and the whole world I scorn, and seek the sky.
Nor can the tragic end of Icarus
relent my flight—it makes me higher go.
That I shall soon fall down and die, I know:
but which man's life can equal such a death?

The voice of my own heart cries in the air:
"Where do you take me, reckless one! Fly down,
for sorrow comes to those who too much dare."
"Fear not," I answer, "the profound abyss.
Undaunted, break the clouds, and happy die,
if heaven grants so bright a death as this."

SOLITUDE

Vales that abhor the sun, proud lofty peaks
that seem to threaten heaven; caverns deep,
whence night and silence never can depart;
air vanquishing with dismal mist my eyes;
steep and high slopes, and rocks precipitous;
unburied bones; grass-covered crumbled walls,
men's refuge once and now so shelterless
as to be shunned by serpents and by wolves;

unpeopled countryside, abandoned shores
where never is the air pierced by man's voice:
I am a spirit doomed to endless tears,
come to deplore my faith within your midst,
and hoping with my long-despairing cries,
if God bend not, to soften hell at least.

AND THIS COLD FOUNTAIN

And this cold fountain has clear curling waves,
and all about it grass is blooming green;
the plane tree with its boughs, the ash and willow
cast Phoebus out, who hides at times his hair;
and breezes hardly shake the lightest leaves
such is their sweetness in so fair a place;
and the fast-fleeting sun is at its noon,
and all the golden fields are flooding flames.

Upon the humid emerald now rest,
O lovely nymphs, your journey-weakened feet,
so tired and wayworn and sun-scorched are you.
Sleep will give respite to your weariness;
green shade and air, some solace from the heat,
and lively waters will soon quench your thirst.

Galeazzo Di Tarsia (1520-1553)

This tempestuous Neapolitan aristocrat, who died at the age of thirty-three, is an important lyric poet of the first half of the sixteenth century. He was Baron of Belmonte. His vehement attempts to win Vittoria Colonna's heart were unsuccessful. He married Cammilla Carafa whose untimely death is the predominant note of his *Canzoniere*. The Viceroy of Naples, Don Pedro of Toledo, exiled him to Lipari. Back in his native city, he did not enjoy his freedom, for he was mysteriously assassinated in 1553.

The extreme impulsiveness of his nature is manifest in his poetry, which is nervous, violent, rich in feeling, and at times massive and obscure. His sonnets sometimes begin with Petrarchan echoes but end on a purely personal, original note. He is the only poet who can be compared to Michelangelo for some marmoreal quality of his phrase and, especially, for the urgency of his thought. Superior to Michelangelo in rhythm and music, he is inferior to him in scope and imagery. The more one delves into the poetry of the Italian Renaissance, the greater and more genuine sounds the voice of this young Italian poet whose untimely death is among the most unfortunate losses of the literary world.

1

Beauty's a ray that from the primal Good
proceeds, and in resemblances then breaks;
comprises and divides sound, line, and light,
includes and paints what pleases many a mood.
Reaching the senses, then the intellect,
it shows forms cast and fragmented as one;
feeds, and sates not; creates from part to part
desire of self and hope for bliss undone.

Burgeoning slopes wherefrom the east grows bright,
emerald, purple, rubies, pearls and gold,
a resting wave, a dazzling starry height,
the sun's mane, and all other lovely things
are a small shadow of it: 'tis your face
flashes for us the truth's own glimmerings.

2

A man who, won by grievous illness, lies,
feverish, weak, in his old home no more,
but seeks rest under sheltering alien skies,
doubting man's art may still his health restore:
so I, from pomps and ornaments away,
and from rich homes where Love's arm steadier grows,
have come in this lone alpine dell to stay,
seeking once more my solace and repose.

But though I search for thick and stony grounds
where I may only walk and never rest,
forever near me my fierce tyrant dwells:
for if I ride, on the same steed he mounts,
and if I cross the sea, on the same ship
I watch him next to me, his sneer a whip.

3

No feather is so light on limpid air,
nor ship, recently greased, on windless sea,
nor river flowing down from alpine peak,
nor swimmer's feet through open oceans free,
as human thought which, unrestrained, prevails,
along the verdant bottom of its error,
on every bitter precipice of terror,
and on intruding mounts it never fails.

Yet in its quest of the right flash of truth,
a lowly bird unfledged or a slow worm,
a stone, a thorn-bush can quite block its path.
You, then, High Guide, oh, lend me firm and strong
wings for your Truth, and all my flightless thoughts
cut short by showing me where I belong.

4

I crossed the white and icy Alps one day,
ill-trusted hedge of your beloved shore;
now, Italy, I breathe your breeze once more,
and this your air, invigorant and gay.
Ah, it was Love that thrust his wounds on me,
yet I recalled your fatal beauty still,
O shaded valley, O sweet-climbing hill,
which your blind children fail to know and see.

Oh, happy those who, here, amongst you, rate
their wealth one small tilled acre, a small brook,
a dell, an apple, and the smile of fate!
Slumber and peace to me were once a cross
 (Oh, mad, deceitful eagerness of youth!),
and now I am lamenting my own loss.

5

(TO HIS DEAD WIFE)

Cammilla, who in yonder fields of heaven,
lustrous and limpid, one more star arise,
and leave me where no more you soothe my night,
hardly alive and still remembering you;
you come with mercy oftentimes to me,
but wrapped and clothed in raiments of such light
that I can scarcely see you; then once more
you leave my heart in flames, my eyes in tears.

Had he struck both of us, Death would have been
less cruel, and I happy at this age,
unable to retain a fairer thing.
But you, if Death still scorns and shuns my life,
beg, saintly one, the Lord, that I, who plucked you
blossom of beauty, now may woo you star.

6

Lady, who were to me the lively east
of beauty, to my body safe support,
and, strong against the world, a cliff, a port
no wrath of northwind frightens in the least;
now that you fast have fallen to your west,
look down upon this dark and lonesome hill
where I bemoan, so weary and so ill,
your curls of gold and your spent glances blest.

Your death has cost me bitter grief and tears,
but in the midst of this my sundered soul
you see how tears and grief grew with my years.
Oh, it is time in your fair face I found
a different dawn, a different sun, and there
may I then rest, to your sweet bosom bound.

TO NAPLES

O countless happy lovers' happy shore,
O regal ladies' most entrancing site,
elect and memorable source of bright
and varied bliss in years that are no more!
Now you can only boast of woe and war,
of fear, suspicion, cruelty, and fright.
A precipice of tears and darkest night
you have become, which e'en low crowds abhor.

Another face, another fortune Time
once gave you, and I, too, if you look back,
felt in those days as joyous and sublime.
All hope I've seen through these my fingers pass,
and, though in vain and much too late, I know
that every human joy is fragile glass.

Gaspara Stampa (1523-1554)

The greatest woman poet of the Italian Renaissance was born in Padua but spent most of the thirty-one years of her life in Venice, where she was the literary attraction of artists, men of letters, and noblemen. For many years her *Rime* made critics think of a poor, naive young lady abused by a cynical, tyrannical aristocrat. It is, instead, the case of an attractive courtesan who in the midst of her various experiences fell in love with a Collaltino, Count of Collalto, who was too selfishly aware of his military career to be detained by a woman's poetic sighs.

Though sentimental in tone and exclusively feminine in spirit, Stampa's poetry shows sincerity of feeling. Her naïveté, in deep contrast with her sensual passion, is at times arresting and heart-rending. She does not say anything new, yet with the warmth of her lines she succeeds in making the story of her unhappy love part of her reader's life. Her inspiration ranges from audacious outbursts of unorthodox beliefs to deep prayers of repentance and faith in God. Louise Labé and Gaspara Stampa have much in common.

1

I, holy angels, envy not at all
your countless glories and immense delight
and your desire for what can never sate,
you ever being near your lofty Lord;
because too many are my joys, and such
as not to be contained in earthly hearts,
while I before me have those sweet bright eyes
of which forever I must sing and write.

And as in heaven you are wont to draw
solace and life out of his Face, so do
I here from beauty infinite on earth.
In this alone do you outwin my bliss—
your glory's set within eternity,
whereas my own may in a moment cease.

2

O night, to me more limpid and more blest
than all the clearest and most blessèd days,
night worthy of the praises of the best
and rarest minds, and not of mine alone;
of my contentment you have been the one
true giver, and my life's whole bitterness
have rendered dear and sweet, by laying me
into the arms of him who bound me fast.

But I did not become—my only want—
lucky Alcmena, for whom dawn delayed
to reappear much longer than its wont.
Yet I can never sing so well your praise,
O limpid night, but that the very theme
will not outsound whatever hymn I raise.

3

Love, I am swearing by your every dart
and by your sacred and most mighty torch,
that, though this burns me and destroys my heart,
and those darts wound me, not at all I care;
and that, in past and future years, there was
and there will be, of loving women, none—
take whom you please—who might have felt or feel
how those are sharp and this is scorching still:

for of this smarting is a virtue born
that wins and dazzles sense of suffering,
so that it hurts not, or is hardly felt.
That torment which my flesh and soul does gnaw
is but this fear that leads me unto death—
lest all my fire should be a fire of straw.

4

Who does not know how sweetly hearts are stolen,
how sweetly every anguish is forgotten,
how sweetly every longing is appeased,
so that one's soul for nothing else is caring—
let him come here, to his most rare delight,
and listen, O my Count, to you but once,
when, singing, 'tis your habit to make bright
heaven and earth and what is nature-born.

He at the sound of your melodious love
will see the air grow clear, the winds and waves
of every tempest halt and end their pride.
For when he will have seen what you can do,
fully will he believe that with such songs
tigers and bears and snakes were tamed by Orpheus, too.

5

O great endeavor of a courtly knight,
taking along as far as France the heart
of an unwary youthful woman, caught
by Love through the fair splendor of his eyes!
If you had only kept your promises
of soothing with two lines my suffering—
while, Sir, you have been aiming at one goal
all of your longings—gathering new fame.

But in the ancient volumes I have read
that the great heroes did not scorn at all
to follow Venus equally with Mars.
And of the king you follow I have heard
that highly he divides such cares, for which
he's known from western down to eastern shores.

6

So weary from my waiting am I now,
so overcome with anguish and desire,
for the small faith and great forgetfulness
of one who's failing to speed back to me,
that her, who with her sickle makes the world
grow pale and white, and takes our final fee,
I often beg to soothe my misery,
so wide awake is sorrow in my breast.

But she becomes as deaf to all my cries,
scorning my ardent and fallacious thoughts,
as he is to my plea for his return.
Thus with the tears that overflow my eyes
billows and seas to mercy I can move;
but, happy still, he lives among his hills.

7

O countless labors I sustained in vain,
O numberless and futile sighs of mine,
O living fire, O faith, which—I know well—
kindled and froze no other woman so;
O papers vainly penned, or to be penned,
in praise of those beloved ardent arms;
O hopes, you messengers of my desires,
deserving a far worthier reward:

the wind blows all of you at once away,
since with these very ears I now have heard
my wicked lord himself reveal to me
that only when he's near he thinks of me,
but, when he leaves, in one fleet moment goes
the memory of my love from him away.

8

O wicked tyrant, send me back my heart,
which you so wrongly hold and tear to shreds,
and do to it and me that very thing
which to a hind lions and tigers do.
Eight days have passed, one entire year to me,
with neither news nor messages from you—
contrary to the oath you swore to me,
my Count, O spring of valor and deceit.

Why, do you think me Hercules or Samson
able to bear so much distress and smart—
me, young, a woman, with my wits all gone
and, worse than that, left here without my heart,
and without you, from whom I used to draw
all vigor and all strength, to shelter me?

9

The wound, which I believed to have been healed
by both the now long absence and small love
of that wild-mountainous and hardened heart,
much colder than a layer of cold snow,
from time to time awakens and grows warm,
and spurts from time to time moistness and blood,
so that my soul lives once again in dread,
which should now be self-confident and bold.

Nor, should I add more nooses round my neck,
could I succeed in keeping the old knot
from hindering my freedom less or more.
They even say that fire drives fire away;
but you, O Love, who seek my martyrdom,
do not allow, ah, such a thing, in me.

10

My heart would come with you,
as you depart, my lord,
if it were still with me,
since that far day Love caught me by your eyes.

Only my sighs will come with you—my sighs,
for these are left to me
in loyal company—
and my laments and cries.

When these things are no longer at your side,
it means I must have died.

11

Sad and repented of my grievous sins
and of my long-delirious empty thoughts
and of the way I spent in futile love
this short and rapid time of fleeting life,
to you, O Lord, who soften every heart,
transform the frozen snow to warmth again,
and make all harsh and heavy burdens light
to those you kindle with your holy love,

I turn now, begging that you stretch your hand
to save me from this sea, whence vainly I
would labor to come out with my own strength.
It was your will, O Lord, for us to die
so as to save the human seed from death:
O my sweet Lord, oh, do not make me die.

Gian Battista Guarini (1538-1612)

Born in Ferrara, Guarini studied at Bologna and Padua, where he met Torquato Tasso with whose *Aminta* his own masterpiece was to be linked through the centuries. In 1567 he was professor of Rhetoric and Poetry at the University of Ferrara, and, later, entered the court of Alfonso d'Este, who sent him as ambassador to various courts both in Italy and abroad. The extreme irascibility of his character made him many enemies and cost him much anguish. A brilliant diplomat, he served the Savoias of Turin, the Gonzagas of Mantua, the Della Roveres of Urbino, and the Medici of Florence. His own children, then his relatives, last the Jesuits, embittered the last years of his life, in spite of his nomination to Prince of the Roman Academy of the Humorists. He died in Venice, far from his villa in the Polesine region, which he had called "Guarina."

His *Pastor Fido,* a pastoral fable published in 1590, was translated into several languages and was widely imitated throughout the seventeenth century. Guarini's phrase is scrupulously terse, fastidiously polished, and does not lack incantation; but the reader, who is asked to compare Tasso's "O lovely golden age" with Guarini's rendition of the same passage, will know, or feel at once, that the former pulsates with a greater and more fervid poetic originality.

His *Rime* contains some charming madrigals.

From *PASTOR FIDO*

(Act I, Scene 1)

Tell me: if in this fair and smiling season,
which crowns with blossoms and renews the world,
you saw, instead of places all in bloom,
and of green meadows and remantled woods,
the pine, the fir, the beech, and the wild ash
devoid of their accustomed leafy hair,
and with no grass the fields, and with no buds
the hills, would you not say, O Silvio, then:
"The world is languishing, and Nature dies?"
Now, feel for your own self that wonderment,
that horror, which would freeze your heart before
such an appalling novelty. From Heaven
we have received as young a heart as is
our age, and longings that go well with this:
and just as love fits no decrepitude,
so, if resisting love, youth is a foe
to Nature and to God.
Look, Silvio, look around:
whatever in the world is kind and fair
is work of Love. The sky's in love, in love
the earth, in love the sea.
That star you watch up there, announcing dawn—
that lovely light above—
is all aglow with love, and feels the flame
of her own son; and she, who makes men love,
with her own love is bright.
This is perhaps the time
she leaves her lover's breast
and full-concealed delight:
look with what smile she goes and with what light.
Throughout the woods the wild
animals are in love; upon the waves
fleet porpoises, slow whales are making love.

That lively little bird,
which is so softly singing,
and so lascivious-swinging
from fir to beech and back
from beech to myrtle tree,
if given human speech,
would say: *I smart with love, with love I smart!*
But fire is in his heart,
and in his way he speaks,
and his sweet mate well understands his cue:
oh, listen, listen, Silvio—
it is his mate that now
is answering: *With love I'm smarting too!*
Within their pens the herds are lowing: those
are sighs of love, not lows.
The lion in his forest now is roaring:
his is no wrathful cry—
it is a loving sigh.
Everything is in love, in simple words,
except you, Silvio: will you, Silvio, be,
in heaven, on earth and sea,
the only person not at all in love?
Ah, let your forest go,
O foolish lad, forget your flocks, and love.

From *PASTOR FIDO*

(Act IV, Scene 9, Chorus)

O wondrous golden age,
when milk was nourishment,
and each wood, cradle of the infant world;
and flocks untouched enjoyed
their darling young, and neither
poison nor sword cast dread upon the earth!
No turbulent black thought
rose in those days to veil
the sun of deathless light:
now reason, hibernating in the mist
of these our senses, shuts the skies away,
so that the pine, astray,
seeks alien shores upon the shattered sea.

That vain and pompous sound,
that futile argument
of flatteries and titles and deceit,
which with a word unsound
a maddened throng calls Honor, was not yet
the tyrant of the soul;
but to endure distress
for truthful happiness,
to call their faith their law
mid flock and forest was
to all those men, accustomed to the good,
effort of honored bliss,
when Virtue warned: "If this is good, do this."

Mid lymphs and meadows then
playing and dancing were
the burning torches of a lawful love;
shepherds and nymphs revealed
within their words their hearts;

Hymen on them bestowed
the sweetest kisses and the deepest bliss;
one man alone enjoyed
love's lively roses, bare:
the thievish lover ever found them hid
from his unchaste desire or coveting
whether in forest or in lake or den;
husband and lover were one person then.

O wicked age, that veiled
with all your lewd delight
the beauty of the soul, and taught to whet
the thirst of our desire
with modesty of glance,
unleashing then obscenities concealed!
Thus, like a net laid down
mid leaves and blossoms strewn,
you hide lascivious thoughts
beneath the holy shyness of your deeds;
nor do you care (it seems an honored thing)
if love's but theft, provided no one knows.

But you, true Honor, lord of all great souls,
oh, breathe into our hearts
the sense of virtue bright!
O king of every king,
come back to these our homes
which blessèd cannot be without your light.
May your incitement's might
rouse from their mortal sleep
those who, pursuing their unworthy, base
desire, no longer follow you, and are
scorning the honor of our ancient race.
Let's hope, for evil, too, at times can cease,
if in our spirits hope still dwelling is.

Let's hope: the setting sun will rise again,
and often from the sky's most horrid black
the long-awaited clearest light comes back.

MADRIGALS

I

O sweetest nightingale,
your darling mate you call,
singing, "Oh, come to me, soul of my soul!"
No song can soothe my rue,
nor have I wings to fly away like you.
O happy little bird,
how well in your delight
does Mother Nature now reward you! She
denied you knowledge, but
gave you, instead, a joyous destiny.

II

A wandering desirous butterfly
is now my heart in love,
which, as in fun,
playfully goes and goes around the fire
of two fair eyes; so many many times
it flies, flies back, and runs, and comes and whirls,
that in the longed-for light
it's bound to lose its life and its wings bright.
But who for this is sighing,
he's wrong, O dear and happy flame: he dies
a butterfly, a phoenix to arise.

III

Cold shines the moon above,
and round the sun's warm rays goes on forever,
yet warm herself is never.
So this cold star of mine
grows beautiful and bright
around the sun of love that in her glows,
but is herself untouched by loving light.

IV

O eyes, O mortal stars,
source of my every ill,
who sleeping yet reveal
it is my death you crave;
if closed you pierce me through,
open what will you do?

Torquato Tasso (1544-1595)

The author of *Jerusalem Delivered* was born at Sorrento, the son of Bernardo, a minor poet, and Porzia de' Rossi. He started his education with the Jesuits in Naples, continued it at the Court of the Della Roveres in Urbino, and completed it at the University of Padua. From 1565 to 1570 he enjoyed the patronage of Cardinal Luigi d'Este, and, in 1572, the Cardinal's brother, Duke Alfonso II, made him the official poet of his court. Highly sensitive, over-scrupulous, ever in quest of affection, he wrote, the following year, a pastoral comedy entitled *Aminta*, which was performed with great success at the Duke's summer residence of Belvedere, not far from Ferrara. In 1575 he had completed his heroic poem, *Gerusalemme Liberata*, but his mind succumbed to a progressive form of paranoia which alarmed the Court and compelled the Duke to have him committed first to the San Francesco monastery and then to the Sant'Anna asylum in Ferrara. After several years of illness and seclusion, in 1586 he left the horrid prison-hospital and, after various restless journeys, was given hospitality in the monastery of Sant'Onofrio in Rome, where he died. Tasso's unhappy life has been a source of inspiration to Goethe, Byron, Rossini, Liszt, and other poets and musicians.

His literary production is vast. He wrote, besides *Aminta* and *Jerusalem Delivered*, *Re Torrismondo*, a tragedy known to Milton; *Monte Oliveto; Le Lagrime di Gesù Cristo; Le Lagrime di Maria Vergine; Le sette giornate del mondo creato; Rime;* important *Dialogues*, and a number of letters, artistically and historically very significant—to mention but a few of his minor works.

A FERTILE PLANT

A fertile plant, if plucked from its deep roots,
though breezes breathe and sun rays shine on it,
can nevermore renew its branches cut,
nor in its season show its happy fruits.
Thus, out of my own land, and having lost
my hapless leaves, and not the leaves alone,
how can I rise again, or when? I'm like
a useless weight with evil omens cast.

Must I now wait for breath of deathless air
and for the sun's almighty lucent rays
and for the bliss of pure and holy streams?
Can I, transplanted, be still green, and give
fruit to a starving man, or shade and peace
to those who, weary of great anguish, grieve?

THE CATS AT SANT' ANNA

As on the Ocean, when the fiercest gales
rouse all its waters into turbid sound,
the weary seaman in the night uplifts
his glances to the pole where stars abound,
so I, in this adversity of fate,
turn, my sweet kitten, to your holy eyes,
and soon I see two stars above me rise
and guide me through the tempest of man's hate.

Look! There's another little kitten there,
and, oh, the Great and Little Bear are they.
Lamps of my study, cats so soft and fair,
may God still save you from man's whipping, may
you always find some milk and meat to share—
so that I write my verse, make light, and stay!

239

LET FORTUNE WIN

Let Fortune win, if underneath the weight
of all these woes I in the end must fall.
Let her; and of my rest and of my fate
the evil spoil be in her temple hung.
She, who a thousand lofty empires made
humble and equal to the lowest sands,
now boasts of this my ruin, numbers all
my smarts, and calls me vanquished by her hands.

Will she perhaps change style and nature now
that all my laughter's weeping? Does she need
a clearer sign of my eternal harm?
Weep, my sad soul, oh, weep: and make of all
your bitter tears a stream of dark, which may
be, later, the Cocytus of our hell.

TO TIME

O old and wingèd god, born with the sun
and with the stars out of the selfsame womb,
who, flying to and fro on crooked paths,
bring to destruction and new life all things:
my heart, which, ill and languishing, complains,
and can through countless reasonings uproot
not even one of all its thorny cares,
can find no other comforter but you.

Tear off my thoughts therefrom; sprinkle my wounds
with gay oblivion, and chase fast away
the fraud with which all royal mansions teem;
and draw from the deep bottom, where it lies,
Truth, and without a shadow, with no veil,
naked and fair, present her to men's eyes.

240

TO HER LADYSHIP THE DUCHESS OF FERRARA

O Royal Bride, the season's on its way
that lures all eager lovers to new dance,
where in a lovely glow and radiance
throughout the limpid, freezing night they're gay.
Now the young maiden, timorous no more,
lends to her lover's secret woes her ear,
and leaves him hanging between hope and fear,
keeping him in a state of happy war.

Great palaces and ceilings bright with gold
are echoing with song; but I still let
this deep dark prison sound with all my weeping.
Do you ignore my merits, new and old?
Are you your word in such a fashion keeping?
Or is a jail, a coffin all I get?

TO A CLOWN OF DUKE ALFONSO II

Sir, scimitar of Pallas, blast and blow
and cannon, fierce and horrible, of Mars,
in fear of which Typheus deep below
is shaking still, and makes his burden quake—
may the lame smith soon forge you with his hand
such armor as the world has ne'er possessed,
and may his wife, in love with you, now land
a pair of horns into his forehead blest!

Oh, work, then, on your lord, that this my jail
be soon unbolted; or with a strong thrust
tear to a thousand bits hard lock and door,
and on the Martian foes we will prevail,
full-armored you, and shoulder-plated I,
thus sharing steel and feathers evermore.

TO FATHER DON ANGELO GRILLO

I sowed and others reap; I water still
a gentle plant in noble husbandry
and others pick the fruit against my will
while I'm afraid of crying openly.
I bear the weight, and furrow the deep sea,
and others steal my merchandise. Whose hand
rules his just kingdom so? Who succors me
if among rocks I sink or into sand?

I'm older, and now feel my strength decay
and grow more fiercely crushed from year to year.
Ah, no new glory equals all my woes,
nor on Parnassus has the sacred bay
bloomed yet for this my brow. The worse I fear:
feats not my own my trump was doomed to play.

TO GUGLIELMO GONZAGA, DUKE OF MANTUA

Sir, from the precipice where Fortune thrust
me, I fall deep into abysses new,
for no one heeds my plea with kindly rue
or shows a glimpse of love for me at last.
Yes, I can see the sun, but only through
a dark eclipse that veils it, fierce and fast;
I have the fixed and mobile stars in view,
but why is such pale doom around them cast?

From this deep darkness now I turn to you,
crying, "In this my great, unworthy plight,
oh, stretch an arm and raise me with its might.
Oh, from beneath the weight that grieves them so,
free this mind's pinions that encumbered lie,
and far above all crowds you'll see me fly."

TO LUCRETIA OF ESTE, DUCHESS OF URBINO

Your prime I likened to a purple rose
that does not open its fresh bosom yet
either to breeze or sun but, like a sweet
and bashful maiden, in its green withdraws;
and I compared you (for no thing that grows
and dies resembles you) to the bright dawn
that sprinkles gold and pearls on peak and lawn
as dewy in the limpid air it glows.

Your less green age now nothing takes from you
for neither richer veil nor younger grace
can win or equal your more simple sight.
Much lovelier and dearer to our view,
the blossom that unfolds its scented face,
and more than dawn the noonday sun shines bright.

TO THE METAURUS

O small yet glorious son
of mighty Apennine,
more famous for your name than for your waves!
A wandering pilgrim, I
to these your kindly lovely banks have come
for safety and for rest.
May the high Oak you bathe and fertile make
with your soft loving, whereby she unfolds
her branches covering the mounts and seas,
shelter me in her shade;
and may this sacred, hospitable shade,
which in its coolness gives repose and home,
take and enclose me in its thickest core,
so that I hidden be from that harsh, blind
Goddess who, although blind, can see me still,
though far from her I crouch in cave or dell,
and on some lonely path,
unknown and in the night, I tread along;
aiming at me forever, for my smarts
she has as many eyes as she has darts.

Alas, since that first day
I breathed the vital air, and opened eyes
onto this light never serene to me,
I was both aim and play
of this unjust harsh Goddess, from whose hand
I suffered wounds long years can hardly heal.
That glorious, noble Siren knows it well,
close to whose sepulcher my cradle lay:
would I had had at the first blow right there
a tomb or a deep lair!
Ah, from my mother's bosom cruel Fate
snatched me, an infant still. Those kisses, ah,
wet with her doleful tears, I now recall
with sighing, and those ardent prayers borne fast
by fleeting winds away:

no more was I to rest there face to face,
sheltered within those arms
with bond so firm and intimate no more.
Ah, like Cammilla, or Ascanius rather,
on tottering feet I followed an ever-wandering father.

In bitter exile and
harsh poverty I grew, from land to land;
untimely feeling for dismay had I,
for harshness of events and misery
forced my still tender years,
before their season, to mature in me.
Shall I now sing his grim old age and all
his losses? Am I not, alone, so rich
with my own woes as to suffice, alone,
for argument of grief?
Shall I then mourn another than myself?
Already now my sighing fails my will;
and these two copious fountains of my weeping
cannot make tears commensurate with pain.
Father, good father, who from heaven watch,
I wept you—and you know it—ill and dead;
and with my tears I warmed
your bed and tomb; now that in yonder spheres
you're blest, you must be honored by your son:
let all my grief be poured on me alone.
. . . .

From *AMINTA*

(Act I, Scene 2)

When I was still a child, and when my hand—
my tiny hand—could hardly reach so high
as to pluck down the fruits from branches bent
of youthful trees, familiar I became
with the most dear and most delightful lass
that ever let her golden tresses fly
free to the breeze. Say, have you ever met
Sylvia, our woodland's pride, our spirits' flame,
Cidippe's daughter, and Montàn's, so rich
in flocks? Of her I speak, alas. So close
was I to her awhile, between two doves
there was and there can be
no dearer company.
Adjacent were our homes,
but closer still our hearts;
and the same age were we,
but much more so our hearts seemed then to be.
With her I would lay traps and cast my nets
for fish and birds; and with her I would chase
the deer and nimble does,
and mutual was our prey, our happiness.
But while I was ensnaring beasts that way,
I felt myself ensnared—I know not how.
Little by little in my heart was born—
I cannot guess from what mysterious root—
perhaps like grass that by itself does shoot,
a feeling strange and new
that made me long to be
ever and ever near
my Sylvia fair and dear.
And from her eyes I drank
a sweetness new and strange
that in the end would leave
something in me that was like bitterness:
and often would I sigh, and always doubt
the reason for my sighing restlessness.

And so I fell in love before I knew
what love was all about.
But then I knew quite well, and in what way
let me now tell you: listen then to me.

Once in the shade of a fair beechen tree
Phyllis and Sylvia sat, and I with them,
when a most clever bee, that wandered wide
gathering honey through those blooming meads,
turning at once its flight toward Phyllis' cheeks
(those cheeks that were vermilion like a rose),
eagerly bit them once and once again,
for, by the likeness probably deceived,
it took them for a blossom. Phyllis then
started to cry and to lament, unable
to bear the sharpness of the stinging ache.
But soon my beauteous Sylvia said, "Be still,
and do not cry, poor Phyllis, for with some
mysterious words of magic I can heal
your little wound and rid you of your pain.
This secret I was taught some time ago
by wise Aretia, who received from me,
as her reward, that ivory horn of mine,
adorned in gold." This said, she put her lips—
the lips of her most sweet and beautiful mouth—
upon the cheek twice bitten, and with tender
music she murmured I know not what verse.
Miraculous effect! The whole pain ceased
of sudden, either for the magic spell
of those words uttered or, as I believe,
because her lips are such
that they can heal whatever thing they touch.
I, who until that hour had longed for nought
save the soft splendor of her limpid eyes,

and her dear words, oh, dearer much to me
than a slow rill a-murmuring while breaking
its course among minutest pebbles strewn,
and softer than breeze singing in the leaves,
I felt a new desire within my heart:
to bring that very mouth close to my own.
And so, become, I know not how, more shrewd
and clever than I am (look how Love sharpens
one's intellect!), I soon remembered then
a gentle, small deceit whereby at last
I might fulfill the craving of my heart.
Pretending that a bee had bitten, too,
my lower lip, I started to lament,
so bitterly, in such a pleading way,
that her sweet medicine, which my tongue failed
to mention, with my eyes I seemed to crave.
Being naïve, my Sylvia,
pitying my distress,
offered her aid to heal
my feignèd wound and, ah, made soon the real
one much more deep and deadly
the very while she bound
her lips to these my lips.
No bee can from a flower
sip such a balmy drop
as was the honey I that moment sucked
from those dew-fragrant roses,
although my burning kisses,
which my desire almost transformed to tears,
were checked a bit by fear
and bashfulness, and thus
made slower and less bold.
But while into my heart,
mixed with some secret poison,
that fatal sweetness crept,

such a delight I felt
that, still pretending the fierce stinging pain
had not yet gone away,
I bade her more than once
repeat her magic spell.
Ah, from that day my longing and my woe
grew so impatient in me that, no more
able to hold the boundaries of my breast,
they had to burst right out: and so, one day,
when nymphs and shepherds in a circle sat,
and we were playing one of our old games—
into the ear of him who sat beside
each had to whisper some most secret thing—,
"Sylvia," I told her, "I'm in love with you,
and if you do not help me, I shall die."
Hearing those words, she lowered her fair face,
and suddenly—a thing most rare—she blushed,
a sign of anger and of bashfulness;
and only silence was her one reply,
a worried silence full of bitter threats.
She went away, and wanted nevermore
to see me or to hear me: and three times
has the bare reaper cut the ripened wheat,
three times already has the winter wind
shaken the woods' green foliage: and I have,
to win her heart, tried everything but death.

From *AMINTA*

(Chorus of Act I)

O wondrous golden age!
oh, not because with milk
each river ran, each forest dripped its honey;
not for the earth that bore,
untouched by plough, its fruits, or for the snakes
that wandered with no wrath nor poison; not
for lack of horrid cloud
outstretching its black veil,
or for the sky that in eternal spring—
this sky that now resumes its happy glow—
laughed in its limpid light;
or for no wandering bark that brought afar
to foreign harbors merchandise or war.

Only because that vain
and inconsistent name,
that idol of deception and of errors,
that which a senseless throng
in future days called Honor
(and made it of our nature lord and king)
had not yet mixed its anguish and its woe
amid the gayety
of each young flock in love;
nor was its grievous law
known to those souls up-reared in liberty;
only one happy golden rule had they,
by Nature carved: *In your desire be free.*

Then among waves and blooms
young Cupids without torches, without bows,
made joyous carolings;
and shepherds with their nymphs
sat, mingling with their words
whispers and blandishments, and with those whispers
kisses, in strong embraces;

the virgin damsel showed
naked her dewy roses,
which now she keeps concealed beneath her veil,
and the unripe hard apples of her breast;
and often playing in a lake or river
was the beloved sighted with her lover.

You first, O Honor, veiled
the fountain of delight,
denying waves to thirst of love; and you
taught lovely eyes to stay
concentered in themselves,
and keep their beauty hidden from men's view;
you gathered in a net
tresses to breezes flown;
you made the sweet lascivious deeds of joy
both fugitive and coy;
you curbed our speech and made our gait an art;
O Honor, 'tis your fault
if what was gift of Love should now be theft.

And all our pains and tears
are now the limpid proof of what you do.
But you, O lord of Nature and of Love,
you, sovereign of all kings,
what are you doing in these shady woods
which never can contain your greatness? Go,
go to perturb the sleep
of famed and mighty men:
but us, a low and a neglected throng,
let here, without you, live
in the fair customs of our ancient race.
Let's love: for human life will make no peace
with years, and quickly flees.

Let's love: the dying sun will rise again;
but when his little light
is fled from us, our sleep is endless night.

MADRIGALS

I

Here waves are murmuring,
and leaves and youthful trees
swing in the morning breeze,
and amorous birds on verdant branches sing
in tenderness beguiling,
and yonder east is smiling:
behold, the dawn at last
came forth and is now mirrored in the sea,
the sky once more is bright,
and fields are pearls beneath the tranquil frost,
and lofty peaks are gold.
O lovely, longing Dawn!
The air's your messenger; but from you start
the breezes soothing every parching heart.

II

Love bids me love forever
the tender bark that wraps
the trunk and branches of a laurel green;
and the new-burgeoned leaves
wherein the newborn birds
mingle their music with the breezes' words;
and the fresh happy shades
that down from foliage young
with softened slumbers on the grasses fall.
There Love conceals his nets,
nor can he find, when weary of his bows,
a more secluded place for his repose.

*

III

Hours, halt your flight
up in the lucent east,
while heaven onward flies forever fast;
and caroling about
the morning air which out
of the sea rises, slow
this human life and day!
And you, O Breezes swift,
bear all my sighing there
where Laura breathes, and here
bring back her voice harmoniously clear,
so that I may alone
hear it, with you and Love, our lord, around,
O Hours, O Breezes kind.

IV

Never a sweeter ray
does the sun dart in the full-blooming May
than that which makes your roses and Mayflowers
bedazzle at all hours;
and, since past snow and summer they still live,
you have the endless April which they give:
a spring eternal dwells within your eyes—
your smile, the sunrise.

V

What weeping or what dew,
what tears were those I saw
fall scattered from the mantle of the night
and from the faces of the stars, so white?
And why did the pale moon
sow such clear storm of crystal-lucent stars
in the fresh grass's lap?
Why in the darkling air
were breezes heard, as if in sorrow, swirling
around around until the light of day?
Life of my life, were they perhaps to say
that you had gone away?

VI

I wish I were a bee,
O lady harsh and fair,
that, buzzing round, might suck your honey out;
and, as I could not reach your heart, at least
I'd sting your soft white breast,
and in so sweet a wound my life I'd leave
and thus revenge achieve.

Giordano Bruno (1548-1600)

The philosopher of the "heroic frenzy of the soul" was born at Nola in the Campania region. A Dominican for only ten years, a teacher in several Universities for a short time, he was a restless, disdainful, rebellious thinker all his life. Endowed with a prodigious memory, arrogant, impatient, impulsive, he brought the turmoil of his mind from Italy to Germany and from France to England. He taught at Toulouse, Paris, and Oxford, but his teaching made him more enemies than friends.

"Doctor of the subtlest theology, professor of the purest and most innocent science, esteemed in the most renowned Academies of Europe, arouser of dormant minds, tamer of ignorance, neither Italian nor English, neither male nor female, neither bishop nor prince, neither monk nor layman, but citizen of the world, son of the Sun the Father and of the Earth the Mother." Thus he introduced himself to the academic body of Oxford, which he at once despised and called incompetent.

His friend Giovanni Mocenigo denounced him to the Inquisition in 1592. The trial of the heretical monk lasted seven years. In Venice, where he was arrested, Bruno at first abjured and begged for clemency; but, later, in Rome, he upheld his philosophy and, when asked to plead guilty, *consentire noluit asserens se nunquam propositiones haereticas protulisse* (refused, that is, to comply, affirming that never had he uttered heretical propositions). He was, consequently, excommunicated and burnt at the stake on February 17, 1600. Two days after his execution, this bulletin was issued: "Thursday morning, at Campo di Fiore, that wicked Dominican friar from Nola was burnt alive. A most obstinate heretic who, according to his whims, formulated several dogmas against our faith and, especially, against the Most Holy Virgin and the Saints, the wicked one chose to die in obstinacy, and said that he was dying gladly and a martyr, and that his soul would rise with that smoke to paradise. But now he must know if he was saying the truth." The greatest of his philosophical writings are *De gli Eroici Furori* and *Spaccio de la Bestia Trionfante*.

TO AN OAK

O aged oak, spreading your branches out
into the air, and all your roots aground;
no quake of earth nor all the mighty breath
which heaven unleashes through the fierce Northwind,
nor anything the horrid winter hurls
uproots you from the place where, firm, you stand:
you are the truthful image of my faith,
which varied accidents will never shake.

Forever the same soil
do you embrace, make fruitful, and possess;
and through its bowels, upward roots you thrust
which are most welcome to the generous breast:
to the same object I,
also, raise spirit, sense, and intellect.

THE FLIGHT

And who is fledging me, who warms my heart,
who causes me to fear no chance or death,
who broke those fetters and those portals loose,
whence few are freed and once again go forth?
Ages and years and months and days and hours,
daughters and arms of time, and that strong court
which dreads no iron or adamant of sort,
have made me fully safe from his great wrath.

Thus to the air I stretch my fearless wings,
and dread no block of crystal or of glass,
but cut the skies and seek the infinite.
And as to other globes from mine I soar,
and deeper rise through the ethereal field,
behind I leave what others see as far.

TO THE PHOENIX

Mysterious Phoenix, O the sun's one bird,
who equal to the world's your happy years
which you consume in blessèd Araby,
you're what you were, I am what I was not.
I die unhappy from the amorous heat,
but you the sun revives with all his rays.
You burn in one, and I in every place;
I have my fire from Cupid, you from Phoebus.

You have predestined terms
of a long life, but a short end have I,
which through a thousand chasms quickly comes;
nor do I know what I shall live, what I
have lived: blind fate leads me,
but to your light once more you surely fly.

NO OTHER FATE

Never will I about my love complain,
without whose life I happiness refuse;
though for its sake I truly bear all pain,
I only want to want to use my right.
Let heavens be cold or burning, dark or bright,
toward the one phoenix I shall never change.
No other fate or fortune can undo
that knot which death itself cannot break loose.

To spirit, soul, and heart,
there is no bliss or liberty or life
that so might smile, and aid, and pleasant be,
or with more sweetness and more happy grace,
than hardship, yoke, and death,
which I by nature, will, and fate, must face.

'TIS LOVE

'Tis Love, through whom I scan so high a truth,
and who unbolts the adamant black portal,
enters my spirit through my eyes; and, born
to see, he lives, is fed, has reign immortal.
He makes us glimpse what heaven, earth, hell contain,
brings the true copies of the absent near,
regains his strength and, darting straight, then strikes,
wounds but the heart, lays bare what's deep within.

Therefore, look forward to the truth, base throng;
heed my unerring words and, if you can,
open, squint-eyed and mad, open your eyes.
A child you deem him in your narrow mind;
'tis you change fast, and so seems he to fly;
'tis you are sightless, yet you call him blind.

Tommaso Campanella (1568-1639)

Born at Stilo in Calabria, he became a Dominican friar. Convinced by a Jewish necromancer that he was destined to be the head of a Holy Republic and the second redeemer of mankind, he in turn convinced others about his messianic mission, and planned a political insurrection against the Spanish domination. The failure of the conspiracy cost him twenty-seven years of imprisonment in the dungeons of Castelnuovo in Naples. In 1626, the Pope requested and obtained his liberation. While in Rome, he was once more accused of conspiracy against the Spanish throne, and would probably have been extradited back to Naples had he not escaped to France.

A few days before his death in the Dominican monastery of Saint-Honoré in Paris, he asked his brethren to adorn his cell with white draperies; he, then, sprinkled it with aromatic rose essence; burned, perhaps symbolically, a few leaves of laurel and myrtle, and had two torches and five tapers lit about him.

His masterpiece is *Civitas Solis* (*City of the Sun*) in which he describes his utopic republic. In his *Poesie* thought and sorrow achieve a single, memorable incantation.

OF THE CROWD

The crowd is but a big, multiple beast
ignorant of his strength; therefore he'll keep
in silence weight and blows of stone and whip,
led by a weakling child that with the least
shudder or shake he could undo at once:
yet, fearing him, he yields to all his whims.
How much he's feared he does not know: he seems
spellbound by ornaments that stun his sense.

Stupendous thing! he jails and hangs himself
with his own hands, and goes to war and death
for but one coin, who gives his king his wealth.
All that's contained in heaven and earth is his,
but he will never know it; and he strikes
and slaughters anyone who tells him this.

IMMORTAL SOUL

Within a fistful of mere brain I lie,
so famished that the books the world contains
have not yet sated my deep appetite.
So much I ate, and hungry yet I die.
By Aristarchus' mighty world first fed,
and more by Metrodorus, still I crave;
longing and feeling, round the world I go,
and the much more I grasp, the less I know.

I'm thus the image of my God immense
Who girds all beings as the sea all fish,
and is alone the goal of loving sense.
Syllogism takes us, a straight dart, to Him;
authority is alien hand; thus I deem glad
and safe that man alone who breeds, and becomes, God.

MANNER OF PHILOSOPHIZING

The world's the book where the eternal Wisdom
wrote its own concepts, and the living temple
where, fresco-ing its actions and its image,
It decked with living statues the deep and the supernal;
so that, to shun all impiousness, each spirit
might read and contemplate here art and function,
and say, "I fill the universe by seeing
God in the core of every thing created."

But we, souls clinging to dead books and temples,
copied with many a blunder from the living,
prefer these erring things to such a teaching.
Oh, make us see how we away are falling,
O ignorance, and quarrels, toils, and troubles:
to the original, by God, let's hasten!

MEN ARE THE SPORT OF GOD AND
OF THE ANGELS

Our souls, masked on the theatre of the world
by their own bodies and their own effects,
prepared by nature, divine art, to give
before the highest council their one show,
utter and do the things for which they're born;
from scene to scene, from chorus to chorus they go,
disguise themselves in gladness and in woe,
as ordered in the comic fatal script.

They neither know nor can or wish to do
or suffer more than the great Wisdom wrote,
glad for them all, to gladden them in turn;
and when, past all our playing and unrest,
sea, earth, and heaven will take back our masks,
in God we'll see who spoke and acted best.

261

A STUPENDOUS DISCOVERY AGAINST
SELF-LOVE

Credulous egotism made man think
there was in either element or star
(though fairer both and stronger than we are)
no mind or love, but that for us they turned;
that, ignorant and backward, save our own,
all peoples were, and by God's eyes rejected.
To his own home, then, man God's love restricted,
and last he came to love himself alone.

And, not to pain himself, man knowledge shuns;
then, seeing the world against his wishes run,
God's Providence or Being he denies.
Deeming his shrewdness wisdom, he, perverse,
to rule, creates new gods, until he calls
himself the author of the universe.

AGAINST CUPID

The world's been bowing for three thousand years
to a blind Love with quiver and with wings,
who now is even deaf, and scorns to hear,
lacking all ruth, about men's suffering.
Greedy for silver, now he's clad in brown,
a plain and trustful naked child no more,
but a cunning old man; and golden darts,
since pistols were invented, he abhors,

but uses coal and sulphur, flame, lead, thunder,
which with infernal wounds infest men's bodies,
and make their greedy minds both deaf and blind.
Yet from my bell I hear an echoing sound:
"Yield, deaf and blind and many-wounded beast,
to the wise Love of spirits innocent."

HIS OPINION OF DANTE, TASSO, AND PETRARCH

Tasso, the graceful and heart-charming notes
of the two greatest of the Tuscan tongue
fully delight us, for the dress is fair
and honors much their exquisite high thoughts;
but better is the fire within their hearts,
whence to the soul that is by virtue tamed
issues that lovely burning and that flame
which is the life of well-born souls elect.

You equal and surpass them both in diction,
yet by your wings the heart is not yet raised
to Heaven, nor does it feel pricked with right wrath.
Oh, when, ignoring all lost souls behind,
shall we feel lifted by your style away
to the one worthy purpose of mankind?

TO HIS PRISON

As from circumference to center goes
each heavy object, and the way, also,
a timorous and playful weasel falls
into the monster's mouth that swallows it,
so every lover of great knowledge, who
travels in boldness out of deadly marsh
to sea of truth, with which he falls in love,
sets at long last in our abode his feet.

Whether men call it Polyphemus' den,
or Atlas' palace, Cretan labyrinth,
or whether others call it utmost hell—
powerless in this place, this I can tell,
are favor, knowledge, love; I tremble here,
where hidden tyranny holds its citadel.

FROM "PROPHETIC PRAYER OF LAMENT FROM THE BOTTOM OF THE PIT IN WHICH HE WAS IMPRISONED"

It is your task, O Lord,
if you have not created me in vain,
to be my savior now.
For this I night and day
cry out to you in pain.
When will you deem it good I should be heard?
I can no longer trust the things I say,
for these my fetters all about me laugh
and mock me for my praying,
until this moment vain,
and for my dried-up eyes and raucous crying.

OF HIMSELF

Fettered and free, escorted and alone,
shouting I hush, and the fierce Bench confound;
mad to the mortal eyes of this low world,
above, before God's Wisdom, I am wise.
With wings by earth oppressed to heaven I fly,
my soul a-singing in my saddened flesh:
and though my grievous weight now pulls me down,
still on my wings from this harsh ground I rise.

'Tis the uncertain war makes valor bright.
Short is all time against eternity,
and every welcome burden is most light.
The image of my love is on my brow,
and I am sure I shall arrive on time
where with no words I shall be heard forever.

Index of Poets

265